T0208798

MASTERMIND YOUR LIFE

How to Achieve Ultimate Success
In Your Life Today and
In The Future

BILL BLALOCK

ARCHWAY
PUBLISHING

Archway Publishing books may be ordered through booksellers or by contacting:

Archway Publishing
1663 Liberty Drive
Bloomington, IN 47403
www.archwaypublishing.com
844-669-3957

ISBN: 978-1-6657-3351-9 (sc)
ISBN: 978-1-6657-3349-6 (hc)
ISBN: 978-1-6657-3350-2 (e)

Library of Congress Control Number: 2022921133

Print information available on the last page.

Archway Publishing rev. date: 12/06/2022

If you think you are beaten, you are, If you
think you dare not, you don't.
If you like to win, but you think you can't,
It is almost certain you won't.
If you think you'll lose, you're lost,
For out in the world we find, Success begins with a fellow's will –
It's all in the state of MIND.
If you think you're outclassed, you are,
You've got to think high to rise, You've
got to be sure of yourself before
You can ever win a prize.
Life's battles, don't always go to the stronger or faster man
But soon or later the man who wins
Is the man WHO THINKS HE CAN!
—Napoleon Hill

CONTENTS

FINAL THOUGHTS

PREFACE

There will always be a future. Work environments, roles, and responsibilities will change, corporate structures will be altered, and a new way of looking at life will evolve over time. Advanced manufacturing, artificial intelligence, virtual reality, advanced communication mediums, and the migration of persons and companies to other locations within the United States and the world will occur. Work settings will be in person, virtual, and hybrid, and four-day work weeks will evolve. There waits to be seen what the future will bring, but there will always be a place for people to excel and be successful.

Research will provide the development of new drugs, vaccines, and medical advances that will lengthen our life spans and improve the quality of our lives. The challenge of finding a cure for cancer, Alzheimer's, dementia, Parkinson's, and various viruses and psychotic conditions will be on the forefront. And yet we will discover new debilitating diseases and conditions that will require specialized expertise and research to find solutions. Again, this demands leadership! As a part of the scientific method, there will be trial and error, but the goal is a successful solution, led by professionals who see ultimate success for their efforts.

Sales and marketing strategies will continue to be refined and recreated with the advent of technology, but there will always be a need for competent and successful sales and innovative and creative marketing professionals to make it happen and get the desired results. Corporations and businesses of all sizes will require highly educated and motivated leadership.

Now is the time to mastermind your life and make your desire a reality. This is your success story. There is no defined timeline for achieving the level of success you want. It is different for everyone, so do not get discouraged. But there must be a beginning! You may be on your journey already, but you need some additional knowledge, resources, and encouragement to continue. That is the purpose of this book.

There are some basic categories the book is divided into, for a reason. Here they are; success defined, building a foundation, developing your career, going through the process, delivering on leadership, sustaining transformational leadership, a winning methodology, and finally, the future. As you can see, it starts with understanding what success is and ends with the future.

Change is always challenging for individuals and cultures, yet over time, we adjust. We acculturate to new surroundings and consider different points of view. This will happen. But the basic desire of all of us is to have a meaningful and productive life we call successful. We all just want to be successful and happy in life. That is the goal and the real purpose and motivation behind this book.

INTRODUCTION

This book is your journey!

You are the only person who can chart a path for ultimate success!

Mastermind Your Life is designed for you to gain insight and surface new thought patterns in your life. It will not be a step-by-step process where, if you follow all the assignments, you will achieve success or reach your goal. Everyone has a different take on what *success* means, and every goal is specific to your personal life choices. So, what is the source of achieving ultimate success?

The answer is using your greatest asset—your mind!

Do you need to change the way you think? The principles and concepts are the same when you are going through your life, but how we approach life matters! One lesson that has really helped me is listening to other people more with a purpose. To understand who they are, where they are coming from, and what is important to them. In that process, I ask them open-ended questions to gain further insight and understanding. Concurrently, I make a practice now to listen more to myself—my thoughts and reasoning, why I say and do what I do. How I feel. It is a cognitive approach to understanding myself and others.

Herein lies the importance of integrating mindfulness and reflective thought into our lives and careers.

This book is for you to ask yourself, how am I thinking and reasoning the decisions I make? What are the trigger points that work for and against me? What are the key elements for personal and professional success? What systems, resources, and methodologies work for my benefit? Do I have a plan? How do I go from success to significance and have balance in my life? Am I a transformational leader?

When you change your thinking, you will change your behavior, and you will get different results. It always starts with the mind. So where are you at this point in your life?

Join me in a journey to discover a new frontier for personal growth and achievement.

It is time for you to mastermind your life and write your own success!

Let us begin.

SUCCESS

1

Success is not the key to happiness. Happiness is the key to success.
If you love what you are doing, you will be successful.
—Albert Schweitzer

There are people who make things happen, there are people who watch
things happen, and there are people who wonder what happened. To
be successful, you need to be a person who makes things happen.
—Jim Lovell

Success isn't measured by money or power or social rank.
Success is measured by your discipline and inner peace.
—Mike Ditka

Success Defined

So how do we define success? It could be building a successful business, spending more time with family and friends, excelling in your career, or becoming independently wealthy. We each define success differently. But we all want to be successful! You will discover that personal and professional success are not mutually exclusive.

Can you recall when, as a young child, you were asked, "What do you want to be when you grow up?" Depending on your age, you may have desired to do what your dad or mom's career choices were. On the other hand, you may have wanted to be a firefighter, police officer, military officer, doctor, dancer, actor, astronaut, or have your own company—influenced by your interests, surroundings, media, internet, and family and friends. Truth is we all want to *be* and *do* something in life as we grow and mature. However, we need to make sure whatever that choice is, we are equipped for that role in life to be successful.

No matter how old we are, where we are from, or what we do for a living, we all share something in common—the desire to be successful! However, there are some foundational strategies that will help you achieve success in life:

To achieve success, you must have a primary goal. And no matter what your goal is, you must establish and maintain healthy habits that lead to goal accomplishment. One reason so many of us are unproductive and procrastinate is that we are waiting until we want to do it. That feeling, unfortunately, sometimes never comes, unless we are prompted by a major consequence. Waiting to *feel like it* should never be a part of the success equation. Habits turn into routines, and routines make it easier to keep up with all the tasks necessary (whether pleasant or undesirable) to achieve success. Some examples would be completing tasks on schedule, being accountable for your decisions, and being on time. What habits would you benefit from in your life?

List the habits you would benefit from:

1. _____

2. _____

3. _____

4. _____

5. _____

The most practical of all methods of controlling the mind is the habit of keeping it busy with a defined purpose, backed by a definite plan.
— Napoleon Hill

Realize a higher probability of achieving success:

Go beyond the norm. Think big. Think possibilities. Everything that exists today was once an idea that was the result of a vision driven by inspiration. How do you see yourself achieving great initiatives? You have the capacity to create new concepts, new technologies, new and innovative products, and services. What you desire in your personal relationships and where you want to live, raise a family, be a part of a professional association, and have a country club membership is all possible. This is where visualization plays a key role. Do you see yourself achieving great milestones in your life? Seeing is believing and motivates you to take whatever actions are necessary for them to become reality. Set your standards high!

Plan. It is essential that you research and do your due diligence so that you make the best choice for your career and your personal relationships. Aside from developing healthy personal relationships, your career choice is critical to your life fulfillment and providing financial security for you and your family. There is no room for excuses. You make your plans, and you own them. Acknowledge your weaknesses, address them, correct them, and move forward! Excuses have no place in the lives of successful and enterprising people. The fact is increased levels of professional achievement result in a positive self-image, good family relationships, and a rewarding future.

Do not be afraid to fail. Never give up. The very moment you give up, you miss the opportunity for success. Someone else will come along and create the very solution you could have provided that would have led to substantial wealth and contribution to society.

To fail is not to be labeled a failure. You just made the wrong decision. We all have those moments. What we learn from our failures will help us make fewer mistakes in the future and give us pause to be mindful of what we are doing in our lives. As previously stated, there is no room for excuses. You own the decisions you make. Creating a healthy environment where you can excel in your career and family life demands that you always recalibrate your life by seeking solutions, so the outcomes are more positive and successful. Remember, you are the by-product of the decisions you make in your life! Only you can adjust and get better outcomes!

Today I choose life. Every morning when I wake up, I can choose joy, happiness, negativity, pain … To feel the freedom that comes

from being able to continue to make mistakes and choices—today
I choose to feel life, not to deny my humanity but embrace it.
— Kevyn Aucoin

Take chances, make mistakes. That's how you grow. Pain nourishes
your courage. You have to fail in order to practice being brave.
—Mary Tyler More

Failure is simply the opportunity to gain again, this time more intelligently.
—Henry Ford

Never, never give up! Be a person of action. Be persistent. Continue to enrich your life with more knowledge and insight into becoming the person you desire to be.

Find what you love to do and do it! For what do you have a passion? Build on that passion, and it will pay off for you. It is a good practice to always chase the opportunity rather than the money. Talented artists, accomplished athletes, and successful business enterprises did not happen overnight. They were birthed by passion and nurtured by a commitment to excellence—whatever the cost.

If I were to ask you if your liked or loved your life, your career, or your relationship, what would be your response? In that moment, your emotional response would be a dead giveaway. Why? Because if you just go through life *liking* and not *loving*, you will have a basic response of "Sure, I like what I do!" But if your response is accompanied by exuberance, joy, a smile, and action, you demonstrate that you are all in. It makes a difference. You must love what you do and do what you love—period. If your heart is not in it, it will show, and you will not achieve the level of success you seek. Make sure to find the right opportunity that excites you and is aligned with your personality, skills, style, and values.

Do not be driven by the opinions of others. Find your place in life and flourish—not to please others, meet their expectation, and become what others want you to become. Be your authentic self!

Let us face it. Do you not have a good feeling when you are dealing with another individual who expresses true joy in what they do for a living? How about the individual who greets you in a store, coffee shop, or restaurant? Are you not prone to feel good about yourself as well and more than likely do business with that person again? I have always been influenced by an attentive waiter in a restaurant who provides exceptional service. The result is usually an exceptionally good tip—a value-driven expression of appreciation. You have had that same experience many times.

The positive energy you generate builds personal relationships, business connections, and lifelong friendships. We are just attracted to others, and they in turn are attracted to us when we express pure joy in our surroundings. It just feels good to be around people who love what they do, and it shows!

Practice the art of effective communication. Having a good relationship with others and building a network of professionals and personal relationships is essential. Be cognizant of how you speak (verbal), your body language (nonverbal), and written communications. All three impact how you are perceived by others. Remember, 40 percent of communication is about listening. Good communicators focus on the other person's message. They also watch for verbal and nonverbal clues to understand the message accurately. Avoid interrupting, talking over, or finishing the other person's sentences for them. Avoid conflicts if possible. At times, you may need to be open to compromise if it will not completely conflict with your overall success strategy.

Believe in yourself. You have the capacity to achieve your desired success! Do not let discouragement stop you. Press on with determination!

To believe in yourself does not mean you oversell your skills to get an opportunity. When you do that, you will find yourself unable to deliver on your commitments, and the result will be devastating. You damage your self-esteem and create a chapter in your career and personal life that is deficient.

What people miss are the countless struggles and failures successful people experienced until one day, by chance or opportunity, they rose to the occasion and were viewed by their peers and others as being successful. We all have periods of great accomplishment and success as well as seasons of disappointment. That is life!

Remember, you are all you have! You are unique and are here for a purpose. We cannot all be stars, millionaires, gifted speakers, national personalities, or leaders of a country. Success should not always be measured by notoriety in the public domain. The most successful people in life are those individuals who try every day to be a better person—loving, caring for, and mentoring others to a better way of life. However, it is a plus when you also achieve remarkable success that leads to financial rewards and security.

Believe in your capacity to succeed. If you can dream it, you have the potential for realization. Success must be something you can imagine yourself achieving. Remember, your dream must have realistic expectations. Be honest with yourself and do not overestimate your ability.

You will always come across people who doubt your ability to succeed. You must not become one of these people. The moment you cease believing in yourself, your skills, and abilities, coupled with dreaming of possibilities, your dreams will evaporate, and your momentum will cease. Keep dreaming and moving forward with positive energy in your life.

Always remember. Success is as you define it for yourself. Is it the size of your paycheck or having a large office that gets noticed because of its location in the building? Is it the feeling you get when you know you did a great job on a project or the one you get when you know you have helped someone? Perhaps you feel successful after putting in a day at work and coming home at a reasonable hour to spend time with your family. Since each of us measures success differently, you are the only one who decides what it means to you. Your satisfaction with your career is strongly linked to whether you feel you have met your goals, not someone else's!

I find a great deal of wisdom when I align my thoughts with those of Simon Sinek in his book *Start with Why—How Great Leaders Inspire Everyone to Take Action* (Penguin Books Ltd., 2009, page 181). I strongly recommend you secure a copy of his book and make it a part of your personal library. Here I share with you his perspective on achievement versus success:

For some people, there is an irony to success. Many people who achieve great success don't always feel it. Some who achieve fame talk about the loneliness that often goes with it. That's because success and achievement are not the same thing, yet too often we mistake one for the other. Achievement is something you reach or attain, like a goal. It is something tangible, clearly defined and measurable. Success in contrast, is a feeling or state of being. While we can easily lay down a path to reach a goal, laying down a path to reach that intangible feeling of success is more elusive. In my particular vernacular, achievement comes when you pursue and attain WHAT you want. Success comes when you are clear in pursuit of WHY you want it. The former is motivated by tangible factors while the later by something deeper in the brain, where we lack the capacity to put those feelings into words.

Success comes when we wake up every day in that never-ending pursuit of WHY we do WHAT we do. Our achievements and WHAT we do, serve as the milestones to indicate we are on the right path. It is not an either/or—we need both.

The Art of Being Focused

Successful people maintain a positive focus in life no matter what is going on around them. They stay focused on their past successes rather than their past failures, and on the next action steps they need to take to get them closer to the fulfillment of their goals rather than all the other distractions that life presents to them.
— Jack Canfield

Be Focused

One of the primary reasons we do not achieve significant goals in our lives is the inability to effectively stay focused on the goal we are attempting to achieve. First, there is a phrase I once heard that has stuck with me: "drifting thoughts get you out of the zone of effectiveness." That statement is powerful and serves as the foundation on which I build the following steps in staying focused for success.

Use time more effectively. We all get the same amount in our time bank last time I checked: twenty-four hours in a day! We need to first give serious thought to how we use our time to add value to our personal lives and professions. Bill Gates, Mark Zuckerberg, Elon Musk, Steve Jobs, Mark Cuban, and Michael Dell made significant use of their time when they began their initial software and technology initiatives. Jeff Bezos created Amazon and changed the way we shopped forever. Great women such as Katherine G. Johnson, Oprah Winfrey, Sheryl Sandberg, Dr. Mae Jemison, Malala Yousafazi, Michelle Obama, Greta Thunberg, and Melinda Gates have made substantial contributions to the social, culture, and future opportunities for women in our society. Today, these people are regarded as persons of great accomplishment and impact on our economy and culture. In the future, many more creative minds and innovators will rise to the occasion.

Set boundaries. Challenge yourself to reevaluate how you use your time. Learn to say no to too many social occasions and meetings that truly do not add value to your life. As an example, we attend many functions because: a) others expect us there, b) our friends and family just want us there, or c) we have attended an event or meeting on a regular basis because we have always done that—a matter of habit. Do some selective procrastination with your participation in activities and determine those that you need to eliminate. Then focus on those activities that add value to your life and assist you in reaching your goal.

Practice visualization. You must see it mentally, believe it to be a possibility, and focus on the reality of achieving the goal. When you do that, you energize and program your thinking to continually focus on seeing the goal to reality. Following this practice of visualization increases the positive energy flow and further supports your pathway to success. Close your eyes. Do you see yourself achieving the goal you have set for yourself?

Be accountable. You must first be accountable to yourself to be focused. Secondly, it is imperative that you share the goal and stay accountable to at least one other person or support group. If your desire is to lose weight and lead a healthier lifestyle, you would be accountable to your physician, personal trainer, or dietician. In life issues, you may seek a professional counselor, career counselor, or a professional coach. Be accountable at each milestone you set for yourself as you work to achieve your goal. Then, when you achieve the goal, others can share in your accomplishment and be a support to sustain what you have achieved. I always encourage people to celebrate their success.

Avoid Distractions. Consistent reflection will act as a compass that can be used to measure your progress. You will know within yourself what your goals are and what you have planned for their accomplishment. This developed clarity will enable you to focus and not be distracted. Be open to the fact that you may need to make adjustments—but stay true to your course of action and do not minimize the impact of the purpose of what you are trying to achieve.

There is no shortage of distractions in life. Here are some suggestions on how to mitigate the distractions we all encounter:

1. *Control your environment,* your physical and mental environments. Remove everything that is not helpful to your defined objective. Make sure your space is conducive to creating the work environment you desire. Avoid checking emails, responding to texts (turn off your smartphone off), and so on. Anything that you define as distracting should be eliminated. Think! List the distractions and then eliminate them.

2. *Be organized.* Create a routine. Disorganization causes distraction, stress, and inefficiency. Focused individuals do not allow mess and chaos to get in the way of their objectives. If you are not good at being organized, enlist a colleague or good friend to help you. Everything has a proper place. Control the things you can control so you can be free to deal with the things you cannot.

3. *Have a defined method.* Multitasking can be your worst enemy when you are trying to be focused. Really focused people know that multitasking is a sure way to accomplish less work. And the work produced is of less quality. I like to use the spotlight approach. As an example, when you go to a concert or an event, when a specific person is presenting or entertainer performing, a spotlight is focused on them. Your full attention is directed at that moment to an individual or artist/performer. You get my point. Schedule your day. Compartmentalize your projects so you can give them your full and complete attention. That way, you have a higher probability of accomplishment.

4. *Be present.* What we learn from history has value, but what is more impactful is drawing from the past but being present in

the moment. Learn from the past, have a vision for the future and where you desire to go, but be hyper aware of what is happening around you in the present moment. Why? Because it influences how you see yourself in the present moment and how you envision yourself in the future. It is a point of reference and reflection that gives focus to your destiny.

5. *No second-guessing.* One of the most distracting activities in life is comparing yourself to others. It is easy to use others' achievements and progress as a measuring stick for your own. One problem. Everyone's reality is different. When we worry about how we approach life, comparing it to others, it drains us of energy and inhibits our efforts to use our skills, talents, and abilities that will make us successful. Your focus is misdirected to others and not to yourself.

6. *Be persistent.* Once you have started the process to achieve your defined goal, do not stop. Continue the process, implementing the steps I have shared with you. Also, be consistent in the journey. Always remember *success stops when you do.* Never, never, never give up!

Once you have achieved your goal, you must then be cognizant that because of your achievement, you have become a person of influence to others. You are defined as a particularly important person (VIP) or, better still, a very *influential* person. Characteristics of a VIP follow:

> *Vision:* You know where you are going. You exercise visualization and see within your mind where you are headed. The idea or direction is conceived

in your mind. You plan, study, and embrace your direction until it becomes reality.

Integrity: You display integrity with insight and intensity. How others perceive you is key. Where is integrity rooted? Your integrity is revealed in your private world within you, your moral compass, and your God. It is what you stand for and defend.

Purpose: You know why you are here. This is the uniqueness of who you are and the fact that you are doing what you were purposed to do. Driven by purpose, you make a difference in your life and the lives of others.

Remember what I said at the beginning: drifting thoughts get you out of the zone of effectiveness. The best way to stay focused for success is to *stay in the zone of effectiveness*! The process is mind changing and life changing. When you have achieved your goal, you become a VIP. You make a significant positive impact on your personal and professional life and in the lives of others around you.

Remember, you can have primary and secondary goals in your life. Each can be specific to personal and family relationships as well as your career choices. We are always working on multiple goals in our lives, and for some, we devote more energy and time than others. Balance is essential. Again, remember, personal and professional success are not mutually exclusive.

Personal and Professional Interconnection

A profession that completely matches your talent, aspirations and skills is the best profession you can choose. Your personal and professional lives will have to go hand in hand and will have influence on each other.
—Abhishek Ratna, No Parking. No Halt.

Connecting

Personal and professional success are not mutually exclusive.

There is a direct connection.

- *Personal success:* This is what you aspire to achieve for yourself emotionally, physically, spiritually, and in your personal relationships. Examples are being consciously aware of your decision-making process, developing healthy relationships, and achieving healthy living habits, such as exercise and diet. Attending to your spiritual self is paramount, which provides for hope, balance, and security in your life walk.
- *Professional success:* This is what you are striving for in your professional life, your place of work, networking, using education and technology, and developing new skills. If an entrepreneur, it means having a successful company or professional practice. As an individual working for a company, it's making advancements within the organization, getting promoted, and acquiring special benefits because of your success, such as stock options or deferred compensation. For those who seek to move on to new opportunities, landing a

position with a new company would serve you well in your pursuit of advancing your professional career.

You might think of them this way: what you want to achieve at home and what you want to achieve in your career choice.

Personal and Professional Success Are Interconnected

What you achieve professionally allows you to do many commendable things in your personal life.

Success is always tied to goals.

Personally, you desire to travel, be a member of a country club, play golf, send your children to a private school, spend more time with your family, or acquire more knowledge through education.

Professionally, you need to have an income that provides for your family, the ability to acquire desired assets and memberships, and vacation time to enjoy your life's desires.

In a work environment, you might be striving for a promotion. Often, it is not about the money or power but what it allows you to do in your own life. I realize that for some it is about money and power, but at the end of the day, the motivating desire is to have the flexibility—and in some cases, freedom—to have what you want in life. If you have a partner and family, it becomes a personal gain for everyone.

Which comes first?

The answer is simple. Neither!

There are three questions you need to ask yourself before you launch out in your personal and professional life:

What do you want?

What is going to make you happy?

What gives you meaning and purpose in your life?

These three questions are foundational to making positive goals that result in good decisions. I would suggest that these questions be first addressed in your personal life. If your life is full of distractions, you will have difficulty. You will have difficulty focusing on your profession if you are physically and emotionally deficient, have problems at home with you partner and family, or have stressful relationships with other people. You cannot be your best with such conditions. Therefore, you need to organize your personal life first, and only then can you expect your professional attitude to change for the better. Here are some suggestions:

- *Find your inner peace.* What is going on in your mind? Do you have a sense of hope and peace within yourself that enables you to make solid goals and create a meaningful life plan? This is where we get down to the bedrock of who we are. The strongest sense of meaning and purpose in one's life is their spiritual self. Having an active faith, whatever your religious beliefs are, is essential. It gives proper perspective to your hopes and dreams and is the basis for a balanced life. Be more composed and demonstrate self-control. Practice prayer, meditation, and mindfulness on a regular basis. I realize that for some, you may be agnostic or have no religious foundation. In such cases, meditation and yoga may be beneficial. The decision is yours. The fact is you need a core belief system within you that drives your hopes, dreams, and ambitions, resulting in formulating goals that help you reach your success level.

- *Be motivated.* Nothing happens until you do something. That is a fact. Look around you, and you will see the results of bad decisions people make. It is not rocket science. Set the example at home and among your friends and family. Be a considerate and kind person, have healthy eating habits, exercise, get adequate sleep, practice your faith, seek new knowledge, be competitive, and so on. The list is endless.

In your professional life, work hard at what you love and what makes you satisfied. Arduous work results in promotional opportunities, and it encourages competition and builds your self-esteem. In a corporate setting, you gain the trust of your colleagues and your employer. It is a win-win situation. If you have your own company or professional practice, you see improvement in your public image, and people trust your judgment in the products and services you provide. You feel better; therefore, you are a better person personally and professionally.

- *Increase your productivity.* I know we cannot be productive twenty-four hours a day. Our motivation fluctuates throughout the week. It all comes down to setting priorities. Not everything has to be done all at once. As you schedule and plan your day and your week, continuously update your goals in priority order. Then for that top priority, devote close to 100 percent of your focus and energy into accomplishing that goal. You can segment your time as well.

For example, give half of your day—preferably in the morning—100 percent of your energy to that one strategic goal at the top of your list. Then after a break for lunch, address less significant items on your list, and before the end of the day, go back to your priority for one more hour. Give that priority 100 percent of your time and energy for one more hour and then debrief yourself about what tasks remain for that one strategic goal and set out to address them the following morning. Continue this process until that one strategic goal is achieved. Mornings have proven to be the most productive time for most professionals. I must admit this suggested process has worked for me, and hopefully you will find it an attractive way to be more productive. There will be occasions when you have to adjust because of a crisis or change in direction by your company. In summary, make sure you plan by listing your goals in priority order, based on expediency, or a set due date and make reasonable adjustments as necessary, but stay on task! As always, continue to invest in education and certifications where applicable to improve your skills.

- *Create the perfect balance.* Balance is exceedingly difficult but important. Understand that life is a continuum, constantly changing. You are part of that process. Being able to manage your personal and professional lives takes time. As you begin to execute your plans in the work setting, you will notice a calmer demeaner in your personal life. You must draw boundaries to know when to stop work and where to begin with your personal life and vice versa. Keep a check on your personal life, giving time to love and your relationship with your partner. It plays a strong role in your personal development. People who are constantly working and avoid having personal time off eventually run out of patience and determination, as compared to those who know when to draw the line.

Identify those trigger points that prevent you from experiencing a feeling of balance and control and eliminate them from your life, such as (1) overcommitment, (2) no priorities, (3) impatience. You know what yours are. Write them down and begin the process of filtering them out of your life.

Your Trigger Points   Action You Need to Take

1. _____   _____

2. _____   _____

3. _____   _____

4. _____   _____

5. _____   _____

- *Maintain healthy relationships.* It is strongly believed that individuals who are in healthy and fulfilling relationships usually end up being successful at work. The reason behind this observation is that such people always have the right motivation and least pressure when they come home or interact with their close friends. Healthy, happy relationships keep our minds refreshed for the tasks at hand. Whereas individuals in unhappy relationships carry the burden to work, leaving their mind confused, not focused, and incapable staying on tasks and making good decisions. Building healthy relationships is essential in your life. It also helps in building networks and client relationships in the work environment.

- *Money.* Okay, money cannot buy you happiness, but it can keep you from slipping into a very unhappy zone. We work for the money, and our personal lives are how we spend our money. How you spend your money directly affects your professional life. If you are reckless in your spending and do not have a savings and investment plan as well as a rainy-day fund, eventually the pressure will mount. You will start worrying about how much you are making, and that pressure along with your debt will impact you emotionally. It is counterproductive to all relationships. Be cautious about your spending, live by a budget, and exercise good judgment in how you spend your money.

There are exceptions to the interconnection between personal and professional success. In an article, "Professional Success and Personal Success: Two Independent Dimensions" on www.invertedpassion.com, November 16, 2011, Paras Chopra shares her perspective:

> All of us chase after success. For majority of us, success means achieving more in life. A better car, a bigger house, a promotion at job or a fancy watch. This definition of success pertains to what I call as professional success. Most of the

stars, sports people, top shot CEOs and other celebrities that you know are at pinnacle of their professional success. They probably worked very hard to achieve what they have today and are also probably very proud of it. So far, so good.

But there is another aspect of success. I call it personal success. If you compare two people: one movie star and another middle-class office goer, do you really think movie star is more happy than the office goer? Deep inside they both have same happiness scale. In fact, for all the possessions and fame that a movie star has got, he may be actually not as happy as the regular office goer who gets to see his family every day and spend quality time with them. Regular Joe is happy as hell, why should he be ashamed of not being a movie star?

So, personal success is a different ball game altogether. It is completely independent of professional success you have got. In fact, I value personal success much more as compared to professional success. Reason for that is because personal success is much easily achievable. You all have a choice to spend quality time with your friends and family and live a rich and happy life. But sadly, many choose to chase professional success like mad people (rats). We work endlessly to achieve the elusive "professional success," odds of achieving which is very less (just compare number of celebrities out there v/s total population on Earth).

So, given you can be happy with your personal life right now, why would you work non-stop and sacrifice personal life for some professional success. Why should it even matter that you could not become Sachin Tendulkar, Bill Gates, Lady Gaga or Tom Cruise? Just because they are at pinnacle of their professional careers, do you think they more happy than you? I doubt and I am pretty convinced.

So, there are different ways to approach success. Paras's point is well taken. When we sacrifice personal success in living a life with meaning and purpose, with the endless pursuit of professional success, we lose! The purpose of this book is to achieve a balanced interaction between the two.

Be on guard that you do not lose perspective of having a happy and meaningful life and just pursue professional success and develop a narcissistic, detached sense of reality.

2

BUILDING THE
FOUNDATION

If you don't design your own life plan, chances are you'll fall into someone else's plan. And guess what they have planned for you? Not much.
—Jim Rohn

Your Foundation

Without a solid foundation, you will have trouble creating anything of value. Think how important the foundation is to a house or building. If the foundation is weak due to poor engineering or there is no foundation at all, what is the outcome? Naturally, over time, the structure begins to suffer. The structure is unstable. Cracks appear in the foundation. The pressure of the structure will continue to increase, and the results could be a failure of the structure to survive.

How would you assess your foundation, your life? Would you say, like a building, it is well thought out, planned, and developed? Have you suffered some setbacks but have taken some steps to mitigate the damage and improve your foundation going forward? Are you just now beginning the process of planning and establishing your foundation?

Let us evaluate where you are right now. Keep in mind we need to be grounded to initiate any foundational life plan that results in personal and professional satisfaction. Assimilating all the information you can is necessary. We all desire a life reflecting successful accomplishments, based on a thoughtful decision-making process.

The Feeling

One person's definition of success may not be the same as yours. Making a lot of money is nice, but if it does not line up with making you feel successful, you will feel as though something is missing from your life. That feeling can leave you feeling discontented. Society tends to define success in numbers. On a personal level, it can be an entirely different mindset. Being a good parent, getting an education, completing a project, getting a promotion, and providing for your family are examples of how many people see themselves as successful. The ultimate success combination is where the personal and professional accomplishments line up, and the feeling is exceptionally good. That is when your life satisfaction index rises to new heights, and you experience a fulfilling life. How you feel emotionally not only impacts you emotionally but also influences your overall health and well-being.

The Faith Fitness Factor

As Chuck Norris once said, "Exercise, prayer, and meditation are examples of calming rituals. They have been shown to induce a happier mood and provide a positive pathway through life's daily frustrations." Putting it into prospective, prayer is more than meditation. In meditation, the source of strength comes from within oneself. When you pray, you go to a source that is greater than you.

Do you feel that there is a higher power—God—that controls your destiny, or are you of the belief that you are master of your own destiny? The answer to this foundational question is extremely critical. If you believe that you are here for a purpose and that God has a plan for your life, you are therefore secure in that relationship and know that God will guide you in your thoughts and plans. Always keep in perspective you do have a free will, and you will make your own decisions. However, your faith and values should be a foundation to guide you in making good decisions.

Such a faith relationship instils hope and confidence in your mere existence as a human being. It gives you a resource for comfort and peaceful living, even amid life and career events that you have no control over that impact your life in either a positive or negative way. Life is full of adjustments. What you say and do has a profound impact on your ability to experience success and relate to others in a positive and reflective way. You should always think through clearly and consider your decision and actions, how they impact not only you but others as well.

You will notice that I stress the need to always *think through clearly* and consider your path. This is more aptly referred to as *mindfulness. Merriam-Webster's* definition of mindfulness is the practice of maintaining a nonjudgmental state of heightened or complete awareness of one's thoughts, emotions, or experiences on a moment-to-moment basis.

Within this process, you calmly acknowledge and accept your feelings. You are therefore in a more calm and focused state of mind.

According to the American Psychological Association, there are many benefits to practicing mindfulness, prayer, and meditation, including all the following:

- better sleep
- calmer emotions
- increased ability to focus
- increased memory
- greater self-awareness
- increased resiliency
- enhanced ability to safely experience feelings
- reduced stress levels

All these benefits promote wellness, clarity of mind, and a healthy life. Isn't that what you want?

As the master of your own destiny, you only look to yourself and your own self-interests. Your decisions have no consideration for others. You have success on your own terms, but it may not last. Narcissism does not just happen. It is nurtured over time as you seek intensely the personal benefits and rewards of your decisions—even if it results in harm to an individual, company, or organization. The motivation is to win at all costs. That is not a good path to take.

You cannot lead effectively in your personal relationships and in business or corporations where consensus and teamwork are not essential elements to achieving success. Collaboration is essential in resolving conflict, differences of opinion, and plans going forward. If you choose to seek your own interests and feed and expand your narcissism, over time, you will find yourself very alone. Regardless of your accomplishments, you will fall short of a successful ending. There will be casualties along the way.

If you find yourself at this point lacking a strong personal foundation, now is the time for renewal. Self-renewal is a fundamental must at this point. As you refresh your life perspective, be cognitively aware that throughout your lifetime going forward, you will always find yourself readdressing the renewal process to stay on track.

3

DEVELOPING
YOUR CAREER

The difference between great people and everyone else is that great people create their lives actively, while everyone else is created by their lives, passively waiting to see where life takes them next. The difference between the two is the difference between living fully and just existing.
—Michael E. Gerber

Your Career Review

As your plan for your career or seek to make a career change, you need to be honest with yourself. I have always said, seek a career opportunity, build on it, and make the most of it. Do not just chase every situation that comes along to make more money. It is more than money. When you make the right decisions and stay the course, the money will come. It takes time!

29

What are your interests? What do you enjoy doing as a hobby? Are there any industries or companies you have an interest in? What do you talk about most when you think about a career? If your parents are doctors, attorneys, accountants, financial planners, or sales professionals, are you attracted to similar careers? What skills will set you apart as an expert in your field? Is your personality type a factor?

Your first point of influence is your family. Your parents and other family members who exhibited a strong work ethic served as influential role models for your development, especially if they were in a specific professional career and did not deviate from their profession. They believed in continuing education and being active in social and cultural settings. In some measure, their interests became yours as well. The odds are, if you fall into this scenario, you will most likely follow in your parents' footsteps. However, even though your parents and family members were successful in their chosen careers but did not express satisfaction with their professions, you may seek to explore another career path that follows your interests and would have a higher probability of greater life satisfaction.

For others, the appreciation for and attraction to individuals in specific professions who serve as mentors can have a similar influence in evaluation and decision-making. As you think through this phase, always understand that choices are made subject to many influences, such as social, cultural, and environmental. The interactions and combination of various decision-making influences are unique to you as well as your life situation. Always keep in mind that things can change as your learning experiences and external factors do, prompting you to fine-tune and revise your career choice.

What about individuals who did not have a strong parental or family influence or even a mentor? Do you find yourself at a loss for what direction you should go in—either starting your career or seeking to make a significant career change? This is not uncommon. In some cases, individuals just want a job to make a living and pay the bills. That thought process is self-defeating. Why? Because you build a career, whereas the alternative is you work a job. There is a significant difference between a career and just a job! You should always look at an opportunity to excel, develop, and grow in a career that will not only provide for you and your family but also bring you a high degree of life satisfaction and accomplishment.

Now is a good time to think about things that interest you. Start by listing five things you do well. When you do this exercise, make sure you discriminate honestly about the items. You may need to adjust the list in priority order. When you do, you have the first insight into your interest and abilities. This insight will help you evaluate your initial career choice or serve to seek a new and expanded career opportunity. With this list in hand, now utilize some tools/assessments that will help you in this discovery.

Your List

1. _____

2. _____

3. _____

4. _____

5. _____

One approach is making sure your personality, work ethic, and style are aligned with a career that would give you a better chance of success. Personality type and interests are strong factors to consider. A widely used theory to connect career fields and personality types is Holland's Career Typology (www.truity.com/test/holland-code-career-test). This type of theory establishes a system of classification that matches your personal preferences and personal characteristics to job characteristics.

Another resource is the Strong Interest Inventory (https://discoveryourpersonality.com). This is a very extensive report that provides you many options and suggested occupations.

By visiting the O*Net database, (http://www.onetonline.org/find/descriptor/browse/Interests), and clicking on a specific occupation cited in your Strong report, you will gain further insight into a given profession.

Utilizing objective tests such as the Holland and the Strong will help you in your evaluation process. Assimilating all the information you can helps you mindfully work through your options in making your best decision.

The Interview

A successful interview depends on various factors, from what steps you take to prepare to how you conduct yourself in the meeting. You will more than likely have multiple rounds of interviews before receiving a job offer. Each opportunity will require making adjustments. Regardless of the type of interview, there are some guidelines that will help improve your chances of impressing a potential employer.

A job interview is not a test of your knowledge, but your ability to use it at the right time.
—WishesMessages.com

Before the Interview

- If you are able to speak with someone who is currently with the company or has worked there in the past, you will have insight into the company culture and work environment. This type of initial personal inquiry can be pivotal in whether you actually pursue the opportunity. If your contact had a successful work experience at this company or is currently with the company, mentioning that fact in the interview process could be beneficial. If you are inclined to mention this individual, I would advise you to exercise caution. You do not really know how your colleague is perceived within the company; it may not work to your benefit. Gaining insight into the company culture should be your focus.

- Explore the company. What are their most recent newsworthy events, products and service offerings, and position in their industry? Are they innovative, and do they have a consistent competitive advantage? Will you be comfortable endorsing their products and services? Use the internet and company website to learn all you can. Learn as many details as possible about the company so you can ask informed questions.

- Prepare answers to the following common questions:
  - Why do you want this job?
  - Tell me about yourself.
  - Why should we hire you?
  - What are your strengths?
  - What are your weaknesses?
  - What do you know about the company?
  - How did you learn of this opportunity?
  - What is your work ethic?
  - How can you make a difference in the company?
  - What have you accomplished in the past that would add value to this new role?
  - What kind of environment do you prefer to work in?
  - How do you handle conflicts in the work environment?
  - How would your current employer and colleagues describe you?
  - How do you handle pressure?
  - What is my expectation of myself in this new role?

In addition to being prepared by answering these questions, make sure you have prepared some questions for the interviewer. This will show your investment in both the position and the organization. Interviewers always ask if you have any questions. You should always have one or two ready! If you say, "No, not at this time," he or she may conclude that you are not interested in the job or the company. A good all-purpose question is "If you could design the ideal candidate for this position from the ground up, what would he or she be like?"

During the Interview

It's always good to remember the organization has surfaced you as a viable candidate, first because of what you disclosed in your résumé. So you meet the basic hard skills and deliverables for the position, based on your prior work history. Now comes the test—if you can deliver that same confidence in the interview process.

Some studies indicate that interviewers make up their minds about candidates in the first five minutes and spend the rest of the interview looking for things to confirm that decision. First impressions are critical. Come in with energy and enthusiasm and express appreciation for the interviewer's time. Set yourself apart. Sit upright and respond to questions with direct eye contact and confidence. Don't overdo it. Practice to the point that you come across not animated but relaxed and sure of yourself.

Start with a positive comment like "I've really been looking forward to this meeting." (Do not say *interview* since you are establishing a personal connection.) "I think the company is doing great with their product offerings and services. I'm excited by the prospect of being able to contribute."

- Align yourself with the interviewer. You want to establish a personal connection within a relatively short period of time. You might say, "I look forward to learning more about the company and letting you get to know me so we can see if this is going to be a good match or not. The worst thing that can happen is to be hired into a position that's wrong for both of us. Then nobody's happy."

- Be assertive. Politeness doesn't equal passivity. Engage with the interviewer as soon as you meet.

- Be positive. When asked about your last or current job, don't be negative at all. When asked "What did you like least about your previous job?" the response should be something like, "I like my current /previous job very much, but I see this position as the next step in my professional growth, especially with your company."

- Have three key selling points. When the *tell me about yourself* question is asked, how should you respond? This is a classic question. Obviously, you can tell them a lot about your family, interests, and so on. But that gets off message. Focus on your selling points. Here are some suggestions to consider. You need to come up with your own and know each point from memory so you can deliver them in the interview process with confidence.

  o "When I was working for [current or former company], I really enjoyed the company work environment, similar to your company. It was/is a very collaborative environment—everyone working for a common goal."

  o "Our team was successful in completing our assigned tasks in a timely and efficient manner. I love to see our team be consistent in reaching our goals. Being committed is vital."

  o "I believe in being accountable for my actions. Extreme ownership of the decisions I make is very important to me."

Believe in yourself. The secret in acing a job interview is to stop believing in luck and start believing in yourself. Think of your job interview as a battle in which your work experience is your strategy, skills are your ammunition, nervousness is your enemy, and confidence is your ally. The trick to doing well in a job interview is to understand that if you don't get the job, it won't be the end of the world, but if you do, it will change your world!

A good resource in preparation for your interviews is www. interviewsucccessformula.com. Through their website, they provide access to their *Interview Success Cheat Sheet*, which is a summary of textbook questions and how to respond to each one.

Interview Success Formula is an online interview preparation course for job-seeking professionals. The course is designed for people who face intense interviews and want to stand out by delivering impressive and memorable answers that help them land the job they deserve.

Here you'll discover proven approaches that have helped more than thirty thousand people ace their interview, with the help of Alan Carniol, creator of this system. This is an excellent resource!

4

GOING THROUGH THE PROCESS

If you quit on the process, you are quitting on the result.
—Idowu Koyenikan, *Wealth for All: Living a Life
of Success at the Edge of Your Ability*

If you don't know where you are going, you'll end up someplace else.
—Yogi Berra

*The more time you spend contemplating what you should have
done . . . you lose valuable time planning what you can and will do.*
—Lil Wayne

The Process

There are no shortcuts to success. There is and always will be a process of due diligence, personal reflection, testing, and evaluation. We like quick fixes. Immediate gratification. Welcome to reality!

People often tell me that they desire to do what I do. I then proceed to ask them if they have time for me to describe my journey—my life experiences, education, successes, and failures leading to my current role in life. If you have achieved a level of success and desire to go to the next level, you more than likely have your own story. It takes time, patience, and perseverance.

It is at this point that I would like to share with you the life and journey of one of the most prolific and talented artists everyone knows about to some extent. Let us look at the life of Michelangelo! Portions taken from Wikipedia.org / Michelangelo di Lodovico:

Michelangelo was born March 6,1475 in Caprese in a small town known today as Caprese Michelangelo, which is situated new Tuscany, Italy. For generations, his family had been small scale bankers in Florence, but the bank failed. His father then took a government position in Caprese. Michelangelo was raised in Florence. His mother died when he was six years old and was raised then by his babysitter and his father. At this point, his father owned a marble quarry and a small farm. It was here that he gained a love and appreciation for marble.

As a young boy, he was sent to Florence to study grammar; however, he showed no interest in his schooling, preferring to copy paintings from churches and seek the company and influence of painters. Florence was Italy's greatest center of the arts and learning. At that time, art was sponsored by the town council, the merchant guilds, and wealthy patrons such as the Medici and their banking associates.

During his childhood, a team of painters was called from Florence to the Vatican to decorate the walls of the Sistine Chapel. Among that group of painters was Domenico Ghirlandaio, a master in fresco painting. At age 13 Michelangelo was apprenticed to Ghirlandaio. His father persuaded him to pay Michelangelo when he reached 14 years of age. At that time, he was selected one of two painters by Lorenzo de 'Medici, who was then de facto ruler of Florence. He then attended The Platonic Academy, which was founded by Medici. Upon Lorenzo's death, he returned to his father's house and began carving and anatomical studies of humans, which later would provide beneficial to the intricate detail he displayed in his work.

At the age of twenty-four he completed what is regarded as one of the world's great masterpieces of sculpture, The Pieta—a sculpture showing the Virgin Mary grieving over the body of Jesus! This masterpiece is in St. Peter's Basilica in Rome.

Countless other works of priceless art included The Statue of David [1504], The ceiling of the Sistine Chapel [1508–1512], Madonna and Child [1504], The Last Judgement [1534–1541]. In 1546, he was appointed architect of St. Peter's Basilica in Rome. Countless other great expert works of art were created by Michelangelo throughout his lifetime, and he died in 1564. In his later years he took to writing poetry, He was one of the leading influences of the High Renaissance period of art. The Medici family was a great influence throughout many periods in his life.

Michelangelo's heir Leonardo Buonarroti commissioned Giorgio Vasari to design and build The Tomb of Michelangelo which took over 14 years to complete. Marble for the tomb was supplied by Cosimo I de 'Medici, Duke of Tuscany who had also organized a state funeral to honor him in Florence.

As you can see, he found his interest at an early age in marble and sculpturing, and he was encouraged and disciplined in that area. He was educated by some of the experts in his day, and the Medici family believed in him. He was apprenticed at an early age. Perpetually learning was evident throughout his lifetime. From the beginning, even when his father's banking business failed, his father did not retreat but pressed on to another opportunity. Such was his father, an example of determination and drive that more than likely played a part in how he saw his life. Many people saw value in his work but not to the extent it is revered today around the world. His work is priceless and will last for the ages. His legacy is forever. He is considered one of the three giants of the Florentine High Renaissance, along with Leonardo da Vinci and Raphael.

As you follow his life, you see a process unfolding—a gifted interest in art forms, his apprenticeship, learning from his contemporaries and the experts in his time, and his devotion to expressing in intricate detail his masterful works of art. Truly, from success to significance. The process worked!

Success Skills

Business is clear that developing the right attitudes and attributes in people—such as resilience, respect, enthusiasm and creativity—is just as important as academic or technical skills. In an ever more competitive jobs market, it is such qualities that will give our young talent a head start and also allow existing employees to progress to higher skilled, better paid roles.
— Neil Carberry, director for employment and skills at CBI via backingsoftskills.co.uk

Self-actualization is the framework from which we become our best selves!

With permission from Jeff Bogaczyk, *Mind for Life—Think Better—Live Better* (www.mindforlife.org), I share with you his extensive listing of fifty-two essential skills for success in business and life and commentary from his podcast dated December 20, 2017.

Abraham Maslow, a prominent psychologist called this desire to become the best "you," self-actualization, and he put it at the very top of his hierarchy of human needs. It refers to the idea of realizing the full extent of our human potential—becoming the best version of ourselves.

If we think about success in this way, as a journey toward greater personal development to achieve our full potential as human beings, it communicates the idea of "becoming" rather than that of "arrival." Money, possessions, a title, etc., all reflect a destination rather than a pilgrimage and if we think about success as a journey, it changes the way we live and helps to develop a long-term perspective.

A journey takes time. It is not an overnight trip. Many times, we see other people's so-called success and we are tempted to believe we should get there tomorrow. That temptation, especially when it does not happen, can lead to frustration, defeat, and even depression. A long-term understanding of success as a journey of "becoming" helps us to keep going when times are tough. To get up when we inevitably fall. And to have a better outlook on life, rather than dealing with the constant frustration of not "arriving."

Jim Rohn, considered *the* expert in personal development, shared in his essay, "The Miracle of Personal Development," that his mentor once told him, "Jim, if you want to be wealthy and happy, learn this lesson well: Learn to work harder on yourself than you do on your job." This statement reflects the idea of becoming. To get more than you have, you must become more than you are. In other words, unless you change how you are, you will always have what you have.

With this in mind, Mr. Bogaczyk put together fifty-two essential skills for success in business and life. Having studied some of the most successful people, he developed a list of fifty-two skills—one for each week of the year—that are essential for success. These skills are not vocational skills, but they are essential for your vocation. These skills are the "human" skills for success in life.

5 Primary Skill Categories

In an attempt to categorize these essential skills, I tried to group them under some broader and more general headings. Here are the 5 Primary Skill Categories that serve to clarify the fifty-two essential skills for success:

Self-Management—Self-Management deals with what we might call "personal" skills or the qualities that we each possess in and of ourselves. They reflect mindsets or attitudes inherent within us.

Productivity—Productivity addresses the skills needed in order to get things done in a timely manner.

Communication—Communication refers to how we impart or exchange information and meaning. These skills highlight the core competencies around our communicative efforts.

Perception—Perception deals with how we see the world and what we think about ourselves, others, and the world around us. These skills primarily address our intentional and subconscious patterns of thought.

Interpersonal—The interpersonal primarily refers to our dealings with other people. How do we get along with them? How do we manage and think about our relationships, both professional and personal?

Now that we have defined the broad categories, here are the 52 essential skills for success in business and life along with a brief description of each one:

SELF-MANAGEMENT

Self-confidence—the ability to trust and believe in yourself.

Sense of humor—having a light-hearted outlook on the world with the ability to laugh and appreciate a joke.

Living in balance—knowing how and keeping the different aspects of one's life in healthy balance. Understanding how to moderate and realign priorities when things are disproportionate.

Purpose—knowing and living according to the reason you were put on this planet

Risk-taking—the ability to step out on the limb when necessary and not always play it safe. Entrepreneurial thinking and having "guts."

Competitiveness—Having a healthy ambition and willing to get in the arena and go up against challengers and rivals.

Desire to learn—A curious outlook on the world and an unquenchable thirst for new knowledge and new experiences.

Coach-ability—The humility to submit oneself to a coach and the willingness to learn new skills from someone else. Wisdom comes from a multitude of counselors.

Emotional intelligence—a realistic understanding and perspective of one's self that includes self-awareness, empathy, emotional self-regulation, social skills, and motivation.

Grit—the resilience, commitment, and diligence to work hard and keep going during the tough times.

Enthusiasm—a passion for life and the inherent motivation to take on new challenges with determination.

Ethics—Honesty and truthfulness in your work, life, and relationships. Having a conscientiousness in keeping your promises.

Friendliness—Having a general kindness toward other people. This isn't simply being "nice" for the sake of having someone like you, but a deep goodness and charity toward others.

Adaptability—Having the versatility and flexibility to adjust to new conditions and environments.

Authenticity—Being real. Not pretending, grandstanding, or posturing for gain.

Assertiveness—being self-assured and confident without being aggressive. The ability to communicate with confidence and skill the full range of your thoughts and emotions.

PRODUCTIVITY

Research skills—The ability to know how to find out authoritative information about things when necessary.

Goal setting—Understanding how to set goals that are challenging yet realistic. Knowing how to define these in specific ways so they can be measured.

Time management—The discipline to plan your life intentionally and manage the hours you are given each day.

Delegation—An understanding of priorities and a realization of who to assign tasks to so they can be accomplished in a timely manner. This also requires the people skills to assign these tasks with tact, confidence, and integrity.

Attention to detail—Being able to see the trees within the overall forest and knowing the importance of each one and why each particular one is important and must be addressed.

Effective decision making—The skill of making wise decisions that benefit the organization and move things forward. The courage to make the tough call when you feel it is the right call even in the face of adversity.

Crisis management—An understanding of levels of crisis. Knowing the difference between what is really dangerous for the organization and what may be a simple bump in the road and then knowing the proper ways to address each according to its level of importance.

Stress management—The ability to manage stress in a healthy way, to roll with the punches while not accepting the status quo and a recognition and tolerance of the universal and unending context and environment of change and uncertainty.

COMMUNICATION

Presentation skills—The ability to present a message, cast vision, and communicate direction on particular projects to various audiences and in various contexts.

Storytelling—Understanding how narratives give and guide meaning and being effective at weaving those narratives into organizational and interpersonal cultures and contexts effectively.

Public speaking—The skill of speaking in front of audiences confidently and effectively.

Body language—An understanding of the non-verbal messages that communicate up to 93% of meaning in interpersonal relationships. Knowing how to read these messages in other people and understanding how to use your own body language in such a way as to align it with your authentic self and your overriding message.

Listening—The skill of being able to authentically "hear" what other people are saying when they speak to you without inserting your own agenda. Hearing in such a way as to put yourself in someone else's shoes.

Facilitation of discussion—The skill of asking questions and managing a discussion in order to keep it on track, avoid rabbit trails, and arrive at a solution/destination that benefits the organization and allows everyone to feel heard and valued.

Persuasion—The ability to use one's own character, passion, and logic in order to persuade and influence other people to your thoughts and ideas.

Constructive criticism—Knowing how to tactfully give real feedback without ego and communicate to others in goodness how they can improve for their own benefit and the benefit of the organization.

Clarity in Messaging—The ability to make oneself understandable and clear when communicating language and vision. This means adapting one's communication and message to the audience and avoiding language and jargon that muddies the message.

PERCEPTION

Critical thinking—Not simply accepting the "party line" when it is given and thinking deeper about the world in a constructive and not destructive way. Not mere compliance.

Creativity—Understanding the creative process and knowing how to employ creative and innovative thinking in order to do things in new ways.

Intuitive Perception—Reading people and situations—The ability to see people as they really are and recognize their emotional states and even their underlying motivations. The ability to realistically see and assess situations and contexts in order to make informed decisions.

Empathy—The emotional skill of putting oneself in someone else's shoes in order to understand and even "feel" their thoughts and emotions. Having a sense of compassion for those in need.

Lateral thinking—Being able to see things from different and uncommon perspectives. Looking at things through different lenses. Knowing how to reframe problems from new viewpoints.

Strategic thinking—The ability to see multiple "moves" ahead. Taking realistic assessments of where the organization is, seeing what the future could, and likely, will be, and taking the steps to address that future strategically.

Problem solving—Troubleshooting difficulties and challenges in order to accurately define the problem and then finding innovative ways to solve it.

Artistic sense—Being able to see things from an aesthetically pleasing perspective. Understanding artistic and design trends and the ability to recognize them and employ them in the organization. Thinking with design and aesthetics in mind.

Technology savvy—Keeping up to date with the latest technology trends, where tech is going, how it works, and how it can be utilized for the organization.

INTERPERSONAL

Negotiation—The art of making deals that benefit the organization and are considered win/win. Knowing how to work with your counterparts to accomplish and achieve your personal and organizational objectives.

Networking—The skill of connecting with other people for mutual benefit.

Team building—The ability to understand team dynamics and interpersonal relationships in order to construct and manage an effective, high performing group of people.

Conflict resolution—Knowing how to manage and resolve conflict situations. Keeping emotions in check, managing difficult conversations with skill, and knowing how to deal with difficult people

Charisma—The ability to draw other people to oneself. The ability to inspire others.

Diplomacy—Tactfully managing difficult and challenging circumstances to maintain unity.

Mentoring—Knowing how to help someone else to become a better person. Not simply lecturing but coaching them forward on their journey. Investing your time into someone else.

Leadership—Influencing others and leading them on a journey to become better people for the benefit of the organization.

Collaborative—The ability to work with other people, get along, and make the project better.

Etiquette—Knowing what and what not to say and do in every particular context and situation.

Soft Skills

Soft skills get little respect, but they will make or break your career.
— Peggy Klaus, author

Hard skills will get your foot in the door. Soft skills will unlock the C-Suite.
— Bill Blalock

Soft skills are defined by Wikipedia as "a combination of people skills, social skills, communication skills, character or personality traits, attitudes, mindsets, career attributes, social intelligence, and emotional intelligence quotients, among others, which enable people to navigate their environment, work well with others, perform well, and achieve their goals with complementing hard skills." The *Collins English Dictionary* defines the term *soft skills* as "desirable qualities for certain forms of employment that do not depend on acquired knowledge: they include common sense, the ability to deal with people, and a positive flexible attitude."

According to career site Zety.com, here are the top ten most important soft skills chosen by recruiters and hiring managers in 2020, in order of priority:

Teamwork
Communication
Time Management
Problem-Solving
Creativity
Leadership
Organization

Emotional Intelligence
Decision Making
Stress Management

More than half respondents in Zety's survey considered Teamwork and Communication to be the most important. To deliver the absolute best results for your employer you must work effectively with your colleagues. And, whether it is between colleagues, or with clients, you must be able to communicate effectively.

What are your four strongest soft skills?

1. _____

2. _____

3. _____

4. _____

What soft skills do you need to work on?

1. _____

2. _____

3. _____

4. _____

Now you need to research resources that will help you in further developing those soft skills that you feel need attention. Having a good life, executive or career coach is always a good resource as an adjunct to self-learning through books, articles, and the internet. There are some good resources contained in this book. Make use of them!

Hard Skills

Hard skills are tangible. They come from experience, training, or practice.
—Bill Blalock

Hard skills, as defined by Wikipedia, "also called technical skills, are any skills relating to a specific task or situation. It involves both understanding and proficiency in such specific activity that involves methods, processes, procedures, or techniques. These skills are easily quantifiable unlike soft skills, which are related to one's personality. These are also skills that can be or have been tested and may entail some professional, technical, or academic qualification."

According to career site Zety.com, here are the top ten most important hard skills chosen by recruiters and hiring managers in 2020, in order of priority:

Analytical Skills
High-Level IT Skills
Basis Computer Knowledge
Customer Service Skills
Presentation Skills
Team Management
Project Management
Marketing
Writing
Graphic Design

It is quite clear that in the modern workplace, data and tech driven skills are at the top of the list. More than half of respondents in the Zety survey considered analytical skills to be among the most important hard skills for a potential employee. We live increasingly in a digitized world. Data and analytics take top priority.

The winning combination is always the combination of both soft and hard skill sets. Teamwork and communication aligned with analytics and IT/computer skills will continue to be seen as needed priorities as remote working expands. There will always be face to face workplace environments, but some flexibility working remotely will continue to grow as the "new normal."

Hard skills are measurable and usually obtained through formal education and training programs. Workers with good soft skills can help companies achieve higher levels of efficiency and productivity. Do you have the right combination of skills? What do you need to do now to excel in your career or your future career change? The competition will be fierce, but if you want to go to the next level, you do not have an alternative but to continually educate and improve your skills.

What are your four strongest hard skills?

1. _____

2. _____

3. _____

4. _____

What hard skills do you need to work on?
Your List

1. _____

2. _____

3. _____

4. _____

Now you need to research resources that will help you in further developing those hard skills that you feel need attention. Advanced education and professional certifications are always the best foundation for improving your skillset. Being a member of professional associations and attending conferences and seminars for additional learning are a must. Hard skills are always changing and improving. You must be able to execute with the required skills in order to be successful. Never stop learning.

Attitude and Culture

Your attitude, not your aptitude, will determine your altitude.
—Zig Ziglar

The culture of a workplace—an organization's values, norms, and practices—has a huge impact on our happiness and success.
—Adam Grant

One of the strongest energy forces is passion. You must be passionate, from the heart, so that what you are doing has purpose and meaning. Loving what you do, doing what you do consistently with excellence, and taking pride and ownership in the results you achieve are paramount to your success journey. It must come from deep within you, from the heart. If your heart is not in it, you are just spinning your wheels, going through the motions. You will find yourself not getting ahead. What are you passionate about in your career? Find your passion.

I have heard by some people say, "I hate my job!" "I quit!" What am I hearing?

You may be highly skilled and passionate about what you do and feel that you are contributing, but the culture is caustic. The person you report to is a micro manager and is very controlling. There may be gender preferences at play for recognition and advancement. You hate coming to work every day, yet you are highly skilled. The problem is the culture! The fit no longer exists. It is time to move on. So, you just quit out of frustration. It happens all the time.

However, the worst thing that can happen is you stay with that company because it is a well-capitalized firm and you feel safe and secure, even though you are miserable. Trust me, you will suffer added stress and depression. You will be in an unhealthy environment that will affect you personally as well as your family and personal relationships. The choice is always yours. I have said it many times, if you are not happy in your career, why prolong the pain. Make plans for a change. In that process, take what you have learned from the unpleasant experience and do some serious due diligence as you plan for a change!

WorkStride (www.workstride.com), established in 1999, is a firm that provides its clients with configurable reward and incentive programs, through powerful software, strategic program design, and modern reward experiences. Their mission is to provide the most effective and results-driven solutions, centered around client needs, and reinforce the positive behaviors that produce results and growth.

Meredith Mejia, previous director of marketing at WorkStride, published an article on December 19, 2014, that focuses on "7 Elements of a Workplace Culture." A summary of those elements is:

1. *Everyone understands how they contribute.* No one feels like a cog in some huge machine, performing a rote task with no meaning. Each employee understands the company mission and how they are helping to achieve it.

2. *Employees are encouraged to learn and grow.* A great company culture encourages people to be creative and proactive about trying new things and accepts mistakes or failures as part of the learning process. Internal training programs, seminars, obtaining certifications and advanced education ae encouraged and in some cases the expense is reimbursed by the company.

3. *Everyone can be themselves.* A great company culture must be preserved by hiring people who fit that workplace culture. Diversity is important. Persons of different races, cultures, religions, etc. who have a common work ethic feel comfortable in the workplace. Tolerance and respect for each other is needed for this to work.

4. *Corporate speak is minimal.* Every company has its own lingo of acronyms and product names, but communication should

mostly be plain and open. If it is the norm to call employees "resources" instead of "people," or if "use" is constantly replaced with "utilize" it is unlikely that your company has a truly authentic culture. Excessive corporate speak is usually a sign of a need to sound smarter or more important than one is, and a culture of high performers should have little need for it.

5. *People have fun at work.* It is called work for a reason, but a great culture fosters an environment where people feel free to laugh together and form friendships.

6. *Teamwork happens.* A great company culture creates a collaborative environment where everyone works toward a common vision for the organization rather than solely looking out for themselves. When people hoard information or try to compete with others to get ahead, it is a sure sign of a toxic culture where self-serving behavior is rewarded.

7. *Recognition happens.* One complaint we have heard [or had ourselves] about bad jobs is that people often hear nothing about their performance until they have made a mistake. Great companies make sure that employees are recognized for magnificent work regularly.

As best you can, check out a prospective company you desire to work for by speaking with friends and family who either work there or know people who do. Meet in person, on Zoom, or over the phone, but have that conversation. Honest feedback is extremely helpful. You can also check the company out on www.glassdoor.com as another source of information. Make sure you make a well-informed decision.

Motivation—The Approach

Desire is the key to motivation, but it's determination and commitment to an unrelenting pursuit of your goal—a commitment to excellence—that will enable you to attain the success you seek.
— Mario Andretti

Your Motivation

Motivation is great predicter of success. Motivated people are determined to do whatever it takes to achieve their goals. They possess a growth mindset so that their desire to succeed far exceeds any challenges that stand in their way.

It is not the large decisions you make every day that have the most impact. It is those small decisions that matter most. Act on them every day; however, make sure that they are aligned with your values and goals. Let us face reality. We all want to be more motivated, but unfortunately, many fall short. This may be where you are right now! You get stuck, focusing on your fears, limitations, and the reasons you cannot achieve. That small voice in your head continues to replay the failures and missteps you have had in the past. That inner voice becomes your liability. You are not thinking at all.

Something to think about:

- *All too often, do you go through life just reacting and responding to whatever stimulus comes your way?* Are you taking steps to improve the quality of your life? Often, we allow external influences to impact our decisions without thinking them through. Your mindset is reactive and not in a growth condition. Think about what influencers cause you to react and not think when making decisions.

- *How about indifference?* Do you take the easy way out and take no action at all? You stay in a job or even a reputable career, even though it is not rewarding and fulfilling. Chances are you choose not to expand your professional, social, cultural, or even spiritual experiences. You wind up being the complainer. Down deep, you are not a happy person. You settle for the status quo, and you allow life's opportunities to pass you by. And then you wonder why you never got ahead in life.

- *Creative thinking.* That is where you begin to experience life as living with a purpose. You are motivated to living a life with meaning and purpose. When you see opportunity, you act. You are constantly seeking to improve your life through education, new skills, improved relationships, and so on. You are motivated to act. You experience and exemplify a constant mindset for growth and improvement. You continue to make advancements in your personal and professional life. You win!

Your Belief System

> *Start by doing what's necessary; then do what's possible;*
> *and suddenly you are doing the impossible.*
> — Francis of Assisi

So, what is the greatest influence on your motivation? It is your belief system. Your beliefs can either strengthen or weaken your motivation. It comes down to your mindset. What you strongly believe has a direct correlation to your thinking and thus impacts your motivation!

- If you have a fixed mindset that you will never measure up, that speaks volumes. You feel you are not good enough. Negative energy flows, and the results are not what you desire.

- If you have a strong mindset, you will view your misfortunes and failures as natural events and a healthy contributor to personal growth. When you mentally focus on the good of life, what could be, you generate a positive energy force that motivates you to higher levels of achievement. You seek input and accountability through a mastermind group.

Remember: changing your beliefs will change your behavior, and the consequences of your decisions will either be positive or negative.

What you believe about yourself and how you respond to the world around you have a significant impact on how you look at life and move through your career. Here are the most outrageous beliefs that will revolutionize your life. Your old friends might not recognize you anymore. People will wonder what superpower you possess (and you can send them to this article if you're feeling generous).

They come from www.paidtoexist.com. Go ahead, try them on.

> Belief #1: I choose to believe that my life is an in-credible gift.

> Even if the current situation or circumstances of your life aren't what you'd ideally have now, you can creatively notice the ways you've been blessed.

You may need to start very small by noticing little things you're grateful for. If you can find nothing to be grateful for, the fault only lies with you. You can start simple and small by being grateful for your breath or that you have enough to eat. Over time, little by little, your life situation will shift. Expanding your sphere of gratitude helps you tap into the spiral effect: *the better it gets, the better it gets.*

Belief #2: Everyone I meet is a best friend I don't know yet.

The truth of the matter is, we're all connected. In a very literal sense, we're all from the same human family. So why not *act* as if we are really one? Your relationships will see a new depth and richness when you act as if everyone *is* truly you.

Belief #3: Every 24 hours is the most important of my life.

Right now, you have a choice: You can let this day, this moment, be brand new, or you can wallow in the past and worry about the future. You can make today a blessing and a gift, or you can squander it. When you choose to act as if today is an incredible opportunity to love fully and give your gifts deeply, new worlds will begin to open that you didn't know could possibly exist.

Belief #4: Everything will turn out all right.

It always does, doesn't it? No matter how bad things might seem now, they will surely pass as they always do and under every challenge, every crisis, is a lesson waiting to be learned. Within chaos and compost, opportunities and flowers bloom.

Belief #5: Life is a game to be played, not a problem to be fixed.

When you view all of life as a game, it feels more like play and less like a problem to be solved. Why not view everything, even the most difficult challenges, as adventures with mysteries waiting to unfold? Life is not a problem you need to fix, it's a game to be played to the fullest.

Belief #6: I choose to die having done my best, having given everything.

We will all die one day, sooner or later. Would you rather die holding back, or having given everything and loved to your depth? Every moment is a choice. Consider how your choice feels right now. Stop waiting for the right moment. Give your best right now, however you are moved to do so.

Belief #7: No one really cares about me as much as I think. This is incredibly liberating.

The reality is that while you're worrying about what others think about you, they're worrying about what you think about them. It's pretty comical, actually. The good news is that this is a license to do more of what you want. And while doing so, you'll liberate others to do the same.

Belief #8: It's always okay to ask, and always okay to say no.

If you're not getting your needs met, you probably struggle with asking for what you want. That's okay. We're often taught growing up that we can't always get what we want. But that doesn't mean it's not okay to ask. And it's also always okay to say no. The more you *practice asking*, the richer and more fulfilled your life becomes. Don't believe me? Try it.

Belief #9: By serving myself first, I can better serve the world.

The more you take care of yourself, the greater you expand your capacity for serving others. It's as simple as that. And anyway, if you truly believe that *the world is you*, then by not serving yourself, you're actually hurting the world. Is that what you want? Is that the kind of example you want to set? Serving yourself isn't selfish, it's actually one of the deepest signs of caring for others you can show.

Belief #10: Love is always available when I choose to open my heart.

Even in the most difficult challenges and heart-wrenching tragedies, love is available when we choose to open our hearts. It's only when we close ourselves off and shut down that we restrict the flow of love into our lives. When we choose to open, even amidst the pain, we can feel love's flow and realize that love takes many shapes. Love can feel like grief, anger and sadness.

Whether we're experiencing joy or loss, opening our hearts allows the fullness of love and healing to come through. When you open, even when it hurts, that's when real growth and fullness is allowed to come forth.

The Challenge

What's one belief you'd most like to try on? Relax your assumptions and experiment with trying it on for thirty days to see if it's true for your or not.

If it doesn't move you, at least you've learned something about yourself. If you never try anything new, you only risk your life.

Your Relationships

Relationships feed on credibility, honesty, and consistency.
—Scott Borchetta

We can improve our relationships with others by leaps and bounds if we become encouragers instead of critics.
—Joyce Meyer

How is your relationship with yourself? How you relate to yourself directly impacts your levels of success in your life and how to relate to other people. So let us first focus on you!

Influencers. Many people influence your decision-making process throughout your lifetime. Your first level begins with your parents and your family. They set the foundation for your core values of right and wrong and hopefully are your greatest encouragers.

Your extended relationships, such as friends, professional colleagues, and new and developed acquaintances, are just another source of knowledge and reflection. Those relationships develop over your life span.

Since we all have an instinctive need to belong, we must be guarded that we do not marginalize our motivation and desire to achieve success in our lives by letting others dictate our paths for us. The influence of others is only to the extent that you allow! You decide whether you are going to give yourself permission for others to do your thinking for you. Consider their viewpoint and advice for what it is. It is their opinion and experience. Listen but arrive at your own decision on how you are going to proceed.

Do you want others to be the guideposts for your life instead becoming the person you desire to be? Your motivation should always be to evaluate all your relationships and make sure they are aligned with your goals. If not, move on!

For those who encourage you to seek the best solutions in your decision-making process and who give you honest feedback, stay close to them, always remembering it is your life, not theirs. Relationships are healthy when they support your values and bring you happiness. It is time to not only reflect on what you gain from healthy relationships but also what contributions you can make to help them flourish as well.

The Mastermind Impact

> *Analyze the record of any person who has accumulated great fortune, and many of those who have accumulated modest fortunes, and you will find that they have either consciously, or unconsciously employed the Mastermind principle.*
> —Napoleon Hill

> *A Mastermind group is two or more people working in perfect harmony for the attainment of a definite goal.*
> — Napoleon Hill

Successful people have a habit of always seeking new knowledge and feedback through their trusted group of professional colleagues. Napoleon Hill provided a clear definition of the mastermind concept in his book *Think & Grow Rich*. The mastermind principle is the key to attaining your major purpose in life.

You can launch your own mastermind group without any experience if you are seriously motivated. But it is highly suggested that you seek a facilitator who can lead the group who has experience and framework to make the group effective. The group is like an advisory board as well as mentors to help you in your business and professional career. The key to the group is that every member is an active participant, and each member is accountable to the others.

Benefits of a mastermind group are:

- accountability
- diversity in backgrounds
- broader business experience
- exchange of knowledge
- enlarged network of connections
- creative ideas
- emotional support
- increased productivity and earnings due to shared processes

Groups are most effective when they are small (two to ten members) and have a shared commitment to shared values and desire to achieve greater levels of success. Masterminds are groups where entrepreneurs discuss business. They can be in person, on social media, in video conferences, or other mediums. While some use them to close deals, for others, masterminds are simply an organized way to meet like-minded people.

There are many resources on the internet for how to create and facilitate a mastermind group.

Here are some major mastermind groups that C-level executives and entrepreneurs participate in. They have a proven track record of effectiveness in their process of structure and accountability.

- *Entrepreneurs Organization (EO)—hub.eonetwork.org*

    EO is perhaps the most well-known mastermind brand. Over 13,000 entrepreneurs are members. Each meets the standard of over $1 million in revenue. Meetings are in-person at local chapters with discussions covering business, life, and balancing the two.

    If you meet its requirements EO is very reasonable. The membership cost is minimal compared to other groups. The network is international with members near every major city you can travel to.

- *Business Network International (BNI)—www.bni.com*

    Business Network International (BNI) is the largest and most accessible mastermind. It has over 8,989 chapters and 253,000 members globally. Interaction takes place on social media and in-person at local chapters.

    Along with mentorship and community, BNI coordinates a staggering amount of business. 11.2 million referrals and $15.7 billion deals were closed last year within BNI's network. The sheer size allows for diverse, unexpected partnerships for growth.

- *Vistage—www.vistage.com*

Vistage is a network of executives who meet in person. It is reserved for leaders with over $500K annual revenue in their business. Discussions are sworn as anonymous to stay within the group. The main goal is to cultivate a corporate network of close relationships.

It is ideal for larger startups. Vistage is older and reminiscent of Napoleon Hill's *Think and Grow Rich* generation. This is not to dismiss it. While your start up woes will be less empathized with, expect to learn invaluable corporate tactics at Vistage. If you are a "CEO" not a "founder," it could be the ideal squad for you.

- *Young Presidents Organization (YPO)—www.ypo.org*

The Young President's Organization (YPO) is one of the most impressive mastermind brands. The group began in 1950. It connects 27,000 CEOs globally. Members must be under 45 years of age with business standards like fifty full-time employees and total compensation exceeding $2 million. The setting is intended to be corporate.

Members connect in-person. Events often include speakers like Richard Branson, Steve Wozniak, and heads of state. If you apply for membership and are approved, do not let this opportunity pass.

When you are in a mastermind group, you must be cautious that you do not view that association as an end-all in seeking new concepts, innovation, technology advances, and go-to-market initiatives. You bring that back to your management team, which is a subset mastermind group within your company. You share your insights with the group and seek further input from your direct reports as you do your strategic planning for the organization. With their input, you have buy-in from your team, and the probability of any changes decided by your team will have a higher probability of success.

Mastermind Subset Groups

Within each area of the organization, thought leaders should be enlisted and engaged in periodic mastermind group sessions to advance the plans and objectives of the organization. Participants should not all be senior staff but also managers and front-line workers. There should be no more than eight individuals within a subset group.

Groups would be primarily from the following areas, each with a C-level sponsor. (These are only suggestions. Social service, nonprofits, and so on would have different primary functional areas, which should be the internal framework for a subset group.)

- manufacturing
- marketing
- product innovation and research
- sales
- technology

- accounting and finance
- human resources

Areas of focus for each group would be:

- challenges
- opportunities
- strategy
- testing

Within the context of each of the areas of focus would be metrics, analytics, methodology, and execution, which would be addressed to achieve the best outcomes. The areas of focus would apply to any organization.

Feedback would be upstream through the C-level sponsor to the senior management team in making strategic decisions of product development, innovation, and go-to-market initiatives.

Subset group sessions should be a mix of in person and hybrid. Frequency of sessions is dependent on the size, scope, and complexity of the organization and what the defined objectives of the subset group are. Selection of participants and subset group objectives will be determined by the C-level sponsor with input from senior staff.

Why the subset group? The best information usually comes from within the organization. All too often, organizations engage consultants rather than utilizing the vast knowledge of individuals within the company. First line of effectiveness is to use the talent in which you have invested. You can always call-in consults to review the findings and recommendations of the subset group.

The mistake many executives make is being a part of a mastermind group and not sharing the information gained with their management team. Such executives, in many respects, are insecure, want total and complete control of all decisions, and do not rely on the keen insight of their management team being a part of the process. Many executives of this mindset are usually overwhelmed and find themselves short on time, making uninformed and untested decisions that do not turn out well.

Remember, as a leader in your company, you need to instill confidence and resilience in your management team, always developing them as leaders and charging them to develop their direct reports into effective leaders as well. As a result, the organization is strengthened, and earnings and growth prospects are heightened.

Leaders train leaders to lead, and everyone wins!

The Mentor Impact

A mentor is someone with a willingness to help others, who has a capacity to inspire, a determination to work hard, a clear sense of vision, an inspiring purpose, a deep sense of integrity and an appreciation for joy.
— Kerry Kennedy

Your Mentors

The mastermind mind approach might not be where you are at this moment. Understandably so. That being the case, a desirable alternative would be a mentor instead.

Whether for personal or career goals, mentors play a valuable role in the lives of people looking to achieve new levels of success. A mentor is a person with specialized knowledge who you enlist to educate and motivate you in your personal as well as professional life. In many cases, they are people you know in your career field who have a great track record of success, and you can learn a lot from them.

So, what are the benefits of having a mentor?

A good resource for advice. You have immediate access to someone you can trust in your same field of expertise. This is priceless learning from someone who has learned from their own mistakes and can help you navigate through challenges and not make the same mistakes.

Expand your network. Your mentor, because of their contacts, can introduce you to persons in their network who can enhance the mentor relationship and potentially provide new career opportunities not otherwise possible without such a network of connections.

Become a leader. Your mentor has learned from their mistakes and shares how to avoid going down the same path. Of added value is the shared need for improvement in your hard and soft skills to be more competitive.

Constructive criticism. Friends and family members may hesitate to provide the type of feedback you need to make the correct change in your life.

Encourager. When times get difficult, your mentor can provide encouragement and suggestions on how to make it through the challenges you face. Remember, negative thoughts may become more prominent in your daily life, especially when dealing with a difficult subject or issue. Positive reinforcement helps overcome those challenges.

Unbiased opinions. If you are having to make choices and you want another set of eyes and ears in the process, your mentor can provide great insight in the decision process. They can draw from their past experiences and their knowledge base to help you make the best decision.

New perspective. It's always good to have a mentor who is up to date on current technology and new learnings in your field of expertise and who shares a constructive opinion about how you are progressing in your career and personal life.

Your desire to succeed at times can be overpowering. One common problem is that it causes many professionals to get off track in dealing with new major challenges. Despite the most earnest effort and best intentions, most people need help when faced with such challenges. This is where the mentor enters the scene. This could be a former boss, one of your favorite university professors, or even a close family friend or professional colleague. The setting is usually a luncheon, meeting over coffee at Starbucks, or with one of your favorite beverages at your local bar/pub! We all need mentors in our intense desire for accomplishment and success!

A great resource for mentors is www.growthmentor.com. There you will have a platform of vetted industry leaders with whom you can connect. Their network spans dozens of verticals, company sizes, and other qualifications specific to your needs. It is a great beginning resource. The cost is minimal when you consider you are getting access to many vetted growth marketing and start-up mentors. They offer many resources to help you in your success journey!

The Emotional Intelligence Impact

Emotional intelligence is your ability to recognize and understand emotions in yourself and others, and your ability to use this awareness to manage your behavior and relationships.
— Travis Bradberry

A strong indicator of successful development is your emotional intelligence. You can have all the knowledge, skills, and vision and still not achieve optimum success. What distinguishes the world's more successful leaders is emotional intelligence—the ability to identify and monitor emotions of their own and others.

Emotional intelligence is essential when it comes to building a well-balanced life. According to the World Economic Forum, emotional intelligence was ranked as one of the top ten most important workplace skills, when it comes to what workers need to be successful.

What is emotional intelligence? It includes four domains: self-awareness, self-management, social awareness, and relationship management. Let us look at all four:

Self-awareness. Being conscious of your feelings and motives. You have a keen awareness of how your emotions affect you and others, and you do not let your emotions control you. You understand your own strengths and weaknesses, you operate from your competence, and you know when to rely on someone else for contribution in your decision-making process. Many times, you find yourself frustrated because you cannot navigate and use your skills to reach your objective. Think about that feeling. That is when you are prompted to seek additional knowledge and assistance from your peers and colleagues to make the appropriate decision on a given task or project.

Awareness begins with reflection. Ask yourself these questions: What are my emotional strengths? What are my weaknesses?

Strengths   Weaknesses

_____   _____

_____   _____

_____   _____

_____   _____

How does my current mood affect my
thoughts and decision-making?

_____

_____

_____

What is going on under the surface that
influences what others say or do?

_____

_____

_____

Self-management. Are you able to keep disruptive emotions and impulses under control? This is strategic, especially when you are dealing with a crisis or a pending deadline that you feel you may not meet. Your direct reports and peers will look to you if you maintain a sense of calm and control for reassurance. When that occurs, everyone benefits. Here are some core competencies of self-management for your thoughtful consideration:

> *Emotional self-control.* You stay calm under pressure and recover quickly from upsets.

> *Adaptability.* This shows your agility and flexibility as you face challenges and uncertainties. You find ways to deal with the complexity of the situation and balance multiple demands at once.

> *Achievement orientation.* You have the drive to meet and exceed expectations. You graciously accept feedback on your performance and use that information to facilitate continuous improvement in your professional development.

> *Positive outlook.* You see the best in people, regardless of their shortcomings. Every event presents an opportunity for improved process, innovation, and opportunity.

During periods of extreme stress, do not panic. Take a deep breath, step away emotionally for a brief period, and collect your emotions and your thoughts before you proceed. Accept the context of the given situation and adjust your priorities based on what is important at the time.

Social awareness. This addresses the understanding of nonverbal cues. How are you reading and interpreting other people's emotions? When you are socially aware—especially when dealing with a multicultural workforce—you can effectively relate to diverse types of people, listen attentively, and communicate effectively. Here are some core competencies of social awareness:

> *Empathy.* Are you listening? When you pay full attention to other people, you are listening to them, what they are saying and how they are feeling. Remember, we are always making judgments about other people when we do not fully understand where they are coming from. Put yourself in their shoes. Now how does that feel?

> *Organizational awareness.* Approach situations strategically. Get the whole picture as best you can. As you become more aware of the dynamics of your group, corporation, or client, you can almost predict how they will react in each situation, especially how individuals on your own team will react.

Social awareness requires good listening skills. Do not talk over individuals or try to hijack a meeting or an agenda. Ask open-ended questions and encourage others to do the same. Get as much input as you can to fully understand others and where they are coming from. Also, challenge your prejudices and surface commonalities that can result in a good outcome.

Relationship management. This interpersonal skill allows you to act on ways to motivate, inspire, and create a cohesive team while maintaining important relationships. Here are some core competencies of relationship management for your thoughtful consideration:

Influence. Are you a natural leader who can gather the support and trust from others with ease, creating a team that is engaged, mobilized, and ready to execute at a moment's notice? Draw deep within yourself to express your strategy based on your years of experience, knowledge, and skills that have worked for you in the past. Utilize all the previous characteristics and maximize your input. You are the expert!

Coach and mentor. You create an environment of continuous professional development for your team. Constructive feedback and support are essential. Communicating in persuasive and clear ways so that people understand and know what the expectations are is essential. Remember, people are always watching!

Conflict management. You have a comfort level when dealing with disagreements between individuals and teams and can provide a forum for open dialogue to reach a common solution. You may not always agree on a specific form of action, but you can agree on some components of the process that can get people moving in the right direction. Remember what the objective is. You want to make progress. Plus, once you have implemented some of the agreed-upon decisions, and the group sees progress, the group will be more open for additional dialogue to address open issues and complete the project or task where the disagreements originally surfaced. Everyone wins.

Teamwork. You interact as a leader, group member, or team leader and can work with a diverse group. You share in the responsibilities and rewards of others. You understand the value of teamwork in achieving a common goal that aligns with a defined strategy for the company. An added benefit of teamwork is the continuous professional development each member experiences as they discover new skills, processes, systems, and insight into each team member's contribution.

See yourself as the agent of positive change. Do not be afraid to go against conventional norms or take risks. Every concept, new idea, and approach is worth the effort to effect change and make progress. Embracing the elements of emotional intelligence will result in the people you work with and for feeling inspired, motivated, and connected!

Time to take personal inventory. See what areas you need to address in your life to develop your emotional intelligence:

The following signs indicate that you are embracing and practicing emotional intelligence:

- excellent problem solver
- not afraid to be vulnerable and share your feelings
- sets boundaries and does not have difficulty saying no
- viewed by others as an empathetic, gracious person
- asks open-ended questions
- great listener—curious and open-minded

- can have a good relationship with people in different situations
- able to manage multicultural relationships
- able to dismiss a bad moment and move on
- not afraid to admit mistakes and apologize
- understands their actions and behaviors
- self-motivated and not afraid of change
- accepts constructive criticism without making excuses or blaming others

The following signs indicate a lack of emotional intelligence:

- holds grudges
- cannot move past mistakes
- feels misunderstood—always the victim
- has trouble being assertive or taking charge
- does not handle feedback well
- is judgmental and easily offended
- has difficulty maintaining relationships
- does not understand their emotions, has difficulty relating to persons of other cultures

As you can see, emotional intelligence is especially important in the workplace, but these principles are also highly effective in our personal lives as well. One of the great by-products of emotional intelligence is a healthy self-image and demonstrated characteristics of leadership. Being approachable, influential, and decisive are traits that will serve you well in both your personal and professional life.

Some people are born with the gift of emotional intelligence, but others must learn it. Those who have it need to consistently practice it in everyday life. The ability to know yourself and understand the emotions of others can have a positive impact on your relationships and help you succeed in every area of your life.

If you are interested in improving your emotional intelligence, it is a clever idea to start with an assessment. Here are some self-assessments to consider:

Psychology Today Assessment:

www.psychologytoday.com/us/tests/personality/emotional-intelligence-test

Talent Smart EQ Assessment:

www.talentsmarteq.com/test/

The History of Emotional Intelligence

According to the Yale Center for Emotional Intelligence, John Mayer and Peter Salovey are considered the founders of emotional intelligence. In 1987, the term emotional intelligence did not even exist yet. (positivepsychology.com)

The brilliant idea came about one summer when Salovey was painting his home along with his friend John Mayer. Salovey studied emotions and behavior, while Mayer studied the link between emotions and thought.

While they were painting and working, they collaborated and discussed different theories of intelligence. The two also discussed the concern that certain theories of intelligence had no obvious way of replacing emotions.

As they worked, they talked about the idea of a new kind of intelligence, the ability to understand recognize, utilize, and regulate emotions effectively in day-to-day life.

In a paper that was published in 1990, Salovey and Mayer described a revolutionary new idea – that of "emotional intelligence." This may very well be the start of the emotional intelligence trend.

The idea began to catch on and Salovey proceeded to become one of the field's prestigious leaders, moving the idea of emotional intelligence forward. The Yale Center for Emotional Intelligence continues to explore what emotional intelligence really means. The Center's current director is Marc Brackett. Peter Salovey now serves as Yale's 23rd president as of this writing. He continues to carry out his original mission.

Relationship between IQ & EQ (Emotional Intelligence)

> *People with well-developed emotional skills are … more likely to be content and effective in their lives, mastering the habits that foster their own productivity; people who cannot marshal some control over their emotional life fight battles that sabotage their ability for focused work and clear thought.*
> — Daniel Goleman, *Emotional Intelligence*

Emotional intelligence is the key to professional success!

Daniel Goleman was born on March 7, 1946, in Stockton, California. He is a psychologist, writer, professor, journalist, and motivator. Goleman worked at the *New York Times* for more than ten years, writing about the brain and behavioral sciences.

Goleman's article "Why Emotional Intelligence EQ Is More Important Than IQ" discusses the current practice of our education system, which measures student's likelihood of success based on their GPA, standardized test scores, and college entrance exams, all of which are contrary to multiple studies pointing to a 20 percent likelihood of success when based on IQ itself.

Based on that article, Goleman gives five reasons emotional intelligence helps determine success.

- Your IQ can help you get a job, but lack of EQ could get you fired.
- Delayed gratification is a top indicator of future success. The ability to focus on self-development rather than receiving instant rewards is a sign of high EQ.
- Relationship skills like conflict resolution, respectful communications, collaboration and building trust are important at work and at home. Maintaining healthy relationships can only be done if we can understand and can manage our emotions, can conduct important and sometimes difficult conversations, and can consider the emotions of our co-workers, friends, and family.
- The connection between physical health and emotional health are strong. Approximately 80% of physical issues such as heart disease, obesity and diabetes can be linked to a physical response to stress. Stress is experienced when we are not emotionally comfortable and when not managed can create burn out.

- Low EQ can be linked to unethical and even illegal behaviors. Successful leaders demonstrate elevated levels of integrity and ethical decision making requiring a high Emotional Intelligence [EQ]

Goleman's work with emotional intelligence has changed the way we view the idea of IQ as well. When it comes down to it, having a high IQ does not automatically guarantee success in life.

By the 1980s, psychologists were focused on the importance of other skill sets that may be needed to process information and promote success and leadership. These same skill sets are also important in terms of personal fulfillment and happiness in relationships.

According to Goleman, emotional intelligence is not a thing to be looked for but something that is a part of you and an integral part of your inner self. Goleman's book *Emotional Intelligence* breaks several myths about IQ while proposing a complementary model of EQ.

Emotional quotient (EQ) or emotional intelligence is the ability to identify, assess, and control the emotions of oneself, of others, and of groups. An intelligence quotient (IQ) is a score derived from one of several standardized tests designed to assess intelligence.

Goleman believes IQ tests are designed to screen candidates based upon their ability to process information, as opposed to their likelihood of success.

According to Goleman, the infamous IQ only contributes to 20 percent of our success in life. Considering that, we must ask ourselves, what is happening with the other 80 percent?

The remaining 80 percent is the result of emotional intelligence.

This EQ includes factors such as:

- the ability to self-motivate
- persistence
- control of impulses
- regulation of empathy, humor, and hope

Goleman sees IQ and EQ as skills that work separately, not opposing. EQ is subsequently a strong indicator of success!

For more information on emotional intelligence (EQ), it is origin, development, and testing, go to www.positivepsychology.com.

The Impact of Mindfulness

Mindfulness means being awake. It means knowing what you are doing.
—Jon Kabat-Zinn

The term *mindfulness* is used frequently and is very much misunderstood! Being mindful is not a religious practice or some Far Eastern meditation practice. Mindfulness means maintaining a moment-by-moment awareness of your thoughts, observations, feelings, body movements, and surrounding environment. When we practice mindfulness, our thoughts tune into what we are sensing in the present moment rather than rehashing the past or imagining the future.

To put it another way, mindfulness is straightforward. It suggests that the mind is fully attending to what is happening, to what we are doing, to the space we are moving through. The fact is we often veer from what we are doing in the present moment. Our mind takes flight, we lose touch with our body, and soon we are engrossed in obsessive thoughts about something that just happened or what we are concerned about in the future. That surfaces an anxious emotional response. You lose focus.

Mindfulness is a quality we all possess. You do not have to create it; you just need to act upon it and use it to your advantage. You already have the capacity to be present; it does not require you to change who you are. Solutions that ask you to change who you are or become something you are not have failed repeatedly. Mindfulness recognizes and cultivates the best of who you are as a human being.

Mindfulness is transformative:

- Anyone can do it! It does not require you to change your belief system. Everyone can benefit.
- It is a way of living. It brings awareness to and caring into everything we do, and it reduces needless stress. Just a small amount of practiced mindfulness will make your life better.
- You gain positive benefits for your health, happiness, work, and relationships.

Mindfulness can be achieved while you are seated, walking, standing, moving, and lying down. You can supplement your meditation with yoga on occasion. It is a state of conscious awareness in the moment, a meditative state.

Here is an exercise for your consideration:

1. Take your seat. Whatever you choose to sit on—a chair, cushion, and so on—find a spot that gives you a stable, solid seat with good back support. It should be a comfortable upright position.

2. Where are your legs? If on a cushion on the floor, cross your legs comfortably in front of you. If you are in a chair, it's best for your feet to touch the floor.

3. Straighten but do not stiffen your upper body. Your spine has a natural curve, so let it be there. Your head and shoulders can now rest comfortably on top of your vertebrae.

4. Situate your upper arms parallel to your upper body. Then let your hands drop on the tops of your legs. With your upper arms at your sides, your hands will land in the right spot. Too far forward will make you hunch. Too far back will make you stiff. You are tuning the strings of your body—not too tight and not too loose!

5. Drop your chin a little and let your gaze fall gently downward. You may decide to lower your eyelids. If you feel the need, you may lower them completely, but it is not necessary to close your eyes when you are meditating.

6. Be there for a few moments (five, ten, fifteen minutes—you decide). With eyes closed, take in deep breaths and release slowly. Do these five to ten times. As you do, just focus on your body, your breathing, and relax. Just be in the moment. Thoughts will come and go but focus on mentally expressing gratitude and being in a relaxed state. With your eyes closed, you are not distracted by your surroundings, but they supplement your relaxed state in some instances. Focus inwardly. Relax.

7. Experience the moment. You may even doze off for a brief period, which can happen. In most situations, your heart rate and blood pressure improve, and you are more relaxed

and focused as you awaken. The stress has been minimized or eliminated.

8. That is it. It is not a complicated exercise, but it is not necessarily easy. You just must be mindful to do it as frequently as you can.

Your selection of where you are when you do this exercise can vary—in your home, office, or outside where you can experience the feel of a gentle breeze, birds singing, a babbling brook, or just silence in your special place. To be simplistic, you can just describe the experience as a time-out.

After the exercise, you are less distracted, more focused, and ready to take on the tasks before you. Therein lies the benefit of practicing mindfulness in your life. Mindfulness is complementary to achieving a healthy, fulfilling, and successful life!

5

DELIVERING ON LEADERSHIP

If your actions inspire others to dream more, learn more,
do more and become more, you are a leader.
—John Quincy Adams

Leadership is not about a title or a designation. It's about
impact, influence, and inspiration. Impact involves getting
results, influence is about spreading the passion you have for your
work, and you have to inspire team-mates and customers.
—Robin S. Sharma

Leadership Traits

Many books have been written about the development and practice of effective leadership by such notable persons as John Maxwell, Stephen Covey, and Dale Carnegie. In my research, I found a great summary of the qualities of leadership through an article written by Steve Earley, former CEO of Cross Company in Greensboro/ Winston Salem, North Carolina. With permission, I share the content of his article "6 Key Components to Effective Leadership":

These leadership traits are the most common for any effective leader in any organization. They should be embraced and practiced achieving success in your professional

#1 Honesty and Integrity

Great leaders create an organizational culture built on these two core values and hold all employees accountable to them. Without honesty and integrity as fundamental cornerstones of an organization, they will rarely succeed long term. And creating such a culture starts at the top of the organization. Everyone watches the leader and takes their cues as to what is acceptable behavior.

Effective leaders must also be trustworthy. They are recognized for always telling the truth and for practicing the highest standards of ethical conduct. Subordinates believe them and do not feel that their leader has hidden agendas. Good leaders readily admit their mistakes. Although difficult to do, this shows they are honest and can be trusted.

Great leaders show they have the best interests of the company in mind rather than their own personal gain, by making good on their commitments. They hold themselves accountable for their actions and decisions and encourage their employees to do likewise.

Transparency is also important, even when there is bad news to share. Employees know when things are not going well. Trying to put a positive spin without acknowledging the organization's difficulties will cost the leader his or her credibility. Sharing both the bad and the good creates deeper trust and respect.

#2 Outstanding Self Awareness

A leader must understand their own strengths and weaknesses. All of us have faults and instinctive behaviors that produce unintended results and/or consequences. It is critical for a leader to really know themselves, admit their shortcomings and ask for their help in addressing them. This demonstrates humility and humanizes the leader. No one is perfect and if a leader acts like they are, they will lose credibility and trust. In the worst case they will be seen as arrogant and intimidating.

Great leaders seek and welcome feedback and dissenting opinions. They encourage different perspectives and challenge conventional thinking. They create healthy discussions and debates, but also know when to move the conversations forward. And they can maintain their composure in difficult/stressful situations.

Effective leaders practice servant style leadership, trusting subordinates to do their jobs and providing them the necessary resources and guidance that allows them to do their jobs successfully and efficiently. Obviously, different situations may require different management styles. An authoritative style may be necessary in some situations, especially during a crisis. But more often, a servant leadership style that demonstrates that leaders are there to help rather than simply telling others what to do, produces far better results.

Great leaders demonstrate empathy, show humility, and genuinely care about others. Taking time to listen to associates and their ideas, learning something personal about subordinates and their families and asking for their opinions are wonderful examples of how to do this well.

Finally, getting 360-degree feedback from your team about your leadership strengths and weaknesses is essential to creating good self-awareness.

#3 Vision

Outstanding leaders see the whole picture and do not get too focused on specific tasks or initiatives. They have deep knowledge of related industries/organizations and are seen as strategic thinkers. They often have strong networks and consistently identify important trends early in their life cycle. They are exceptionally good at communicating a vision of the future and getting organizational buy-in.

Strong leaders know their target customers, understand the organization's value proposition and, its competitive weaknesses. They focus on enhancing core competencies of the organization and developing the skills and capabilities that will enhance their value proposition.

They are excellent at establishing clear goals and objectives for the organization, and for their direct subordinates. Importantly, they are also able to provide clear and convincing rationale that supports their vision of the future.

#4 Courage

To have courage requires confidence. The best leaders are noticeably confident in themselves and their ideas, which allows them to be decisive. But they must be able to exude that confidence without conveying arrogance or intimidation!

Great leaders have the ability to make tough decisions and are willing to take risks, even when conventional wisdom would dictate otherwise. They must be willing to stand alone if they believe in their convictions. This is related to their visionary skills, strategic thinking, and their self-confidence.

They are also able to recognize when they need the expertise or knowledge of others and are not afraid to admit it.

#5 Communication Skills

Great leaders do not have to be great orators or exceptional writers. What is required is that they are inspirational and persuasive. They can speak and write to the audience's level, focusing on the WIFM ("What's in it for me"). They communicate in a way that generates buy-in and willing followers. Because if you cannot succeed in doing those two things, you cannot effectively lead.

Good leaders must always be truthful, even delivering the bad news when appropriate. But they exude a positive attitude and are seen as optimistic, even in the most troubling of times.

Even if they do not have a professional background or training in sales, leaders often exhibit elements of effective selling skills. They could advance their ideas in a logical and understandable way to all levels of the organization.

#6 Team Builder

Great leaders must have outstanding team building skills. This requires first the ability to attract and retain top talent.

Every great leader knows they cannot do it alone and that having the best talent enhances the opportunity for success. They know they need to build a team with complementary skill sets and experiences and constantly look to bring in people that know more than they do (this is because they are confident).

Importantly, they also understand that a team performs best when its members have differing personalities and styles, to expand perspectives when problem solving and avoid getting caught up in "group think."

A good leader is often more of a facilitator of the team, able to generate healthy discussions and generate consensus. Great leaders know that if the team believes in, and is committed to a strategy or plan, the chance of success goes up immensely. The team becomes passionate about doing what they said they would do. Conversely, when a team feels that the leader will force them to do what he or she thinks is best, innovation is lost and there is little passion.

The best leaders are highly organized and trust the team members to do their respective jobs. The leader becomes a delegator, setting clear expectations and providing on-going feedback.

Finally, effective leaders regularly and officially recognize others. They are quick to accept blame for failures, even when they may have not been directly responsible. And are just as quick to give others credit for successes rather than themselves.

In Summary

These six fundamental skill sets are found in every individual who has been recognized as being an outstanding leader. But it is equally important to understand that few were good at all of these when they started their careers.

Knowing and admitting one's own strengths and weaknesses is the first step in developing the requisite skill set to become a more effective leader. Next, committing and working hard to improve areas of weakness furthers leadership development. Then finally, asking others for help and feedback is essential to acquiring all the necessary skills and traits required to become an effective leader.

What you think, you become, what you feel, you attract, what you imagine, you create.
—Buddha

The Future of Leadership

With permission, I share with you future trends in leadership from author, speaker, and futurist Jacob Morgan (www.thefuture-organization.com). He is a contributor to the *Wall Street Journal*, *Forbes*, CNN, *INC* magazine, and *USA Today*. In addition, he is also the host of *The Future of Work* podcast.:

Will leaders of 2030 be that different than leaders of today? And if so, how? It's a question I posed to more than 140 CEOs around the world for my new book, *The Future Leader.* These included the CEOs of companies like Oracle, Best Buy, Unilever, MasterCard, Verizon, Kaiser, and many others around the world. The consensus is that while some core aspects of leadership will remain the same, such as setting a vision and executing on strategy, we will need a new type of leader to guide us through the next decade and beyond. But why?

These six trends will play a major role in shaping future leaders over the next decade and beyond.

AI AND TECHNOLOGY

When I asked CEOs what they viewed as the biggest trends impacting leadership, the most common answer I received was the growth of artificial intelligence and technology. It's no secret that technology is evolving at a breathtaking pace. Artificial intelligence has the power to completely transform how businesses operate and people work. But with the excitement of AI and new technology comes fear and uncertainty. It's up to leaders to assuage those fears by looking for ways to implement AI that adds to employees instead of replacing their jobs. Leaders need to calm fears and remain positive about new technology. They need to be well-versed on AI and experiment with new technologies so they can help others understand the potential impact on their jobs.

PACE OF CHANGE

Right alongside the growth of AI and technology is the overall pace of change. How we live and work is drastically different today from what it was five years ago—let alone 20 or 30 years ago. Change surrounds us in the form of climate change, globalization, diversity, and dozens of other things. Change is constant and has always happened. What's different about today is the rate at which change occurs. To be successful, organizations must be constantly looking forward, and leaders must lean in and embrace change instead of shying away. Future leaders need to be agile, easily adaptable, and comfortable challenging the status quo.

PURPOSE AND MEANING

While companies used to be able to easily attract top talent with the promise of a high salary, that's no longer the case. Employees now want to work for an organization that offers purpose and meaning, and they're even willing to take a pay cut to get it. Purpose is the reason for an organization's existence and often includes things like investing in employees, making a difference in the world, or driving innovation. Meaning is the personal impact of each employee's work. Employees want to see that their efforts are impactful and contributing to the overall purpose of the company. To set the example, leaders must first understand their own job, purpose, impact, and meaning before helping their employees do the same. They need to get to know employees individually to understand what motivates them.

NEW TALENT LANDSCAPE

Recent years have brought tremendous change to the overall talent landscape, and it's only just beginning. As older employees retire and younger generations enter the workforce, many companies find themselves on the constant hunt for skilled employees. At the same time, diversity and inclusion are becoming even more important. The new talent landscape is more than just changing demographics; it's a new approach to attracting and retaining talent while also training and upskilling employees to be prepared for the future of work. Leaders of the future should strive to develop diverse teams and create an inclusive environment. They need to invest in upskilling employees while also finding ways to involve older employees and motivating employees of all ages to take control of their own career development.

MORALITY, ETHICS, AND TRANSPARENCY

Gone are the days of controlling leaders trying to be the smartest person in the room. A recent push for morality, ethics, and transparency has led to more authentic and humble leaders. Companies with ethical foundations perform better financially and have higher customer and employee satisfaction. These types of organizations are created by moral leaders. At the same time, leaders are being put under a microscope as people demand transparency. Leaders can no longer hide behind their title—they must be open and honest to their companies and the public. Leaders of the future must determine their own moral compasses and have a strong sense of their personal beliefs. Simply standing still is no longer good enough; leaders need to take a stand and be as transparent and authentic as possible.

GLOBALIZATION

As technology grows, the world becomes more connected and seems smaller. Each country used to be its own economy, but now we can work with and communicate instantly with people all over the world. All businesses are now global and have the potential for worldwide employees and customers. Globalization brings complex geo-political issues and great opportunities to collaborate and share cultures. Future leaders need to embrace globalization by becoming global citizens who appreciate different cultures and know how to communicate across cultural and language barriers. Foreign ideas should be viewed as opportunities, not fear-filled challenges. Leaders of the future need to pay attention to global issues and understand what is happening around the world.

Future-ready leaders need to understand trends and adapt their leadership approach for changes in the way we think, work, and live. These six trends will be crucial for leaders in coming years.

Key Principles of Leadership

Must be calm and not on autopilot, reacting to every event. It is normal to show emotion. People need to know that you care about their best interests, at the same time controlling their emotions.

Must be confident but not overconfident. Overconfidence causes complacency and arrogance. Good, healthy confidence is contagious and gives each member of your team increased self-confidence to accomplish the task at hand. There is a higher probability of a positive outcome.

Must lead but be willing to follow if someone on the team has specialized expertise that the leader does not have. Leaders lead, and others facilitate leadership within the team. A great leader recognizes this within their leadership team. Everyone is set up to win!

Must be aggressive but not overbearing. If you are overbearing, others may feel reluctant to approach you with new ideas, concepts, and strategies that would help the team. Listen to your team, and they will have more confidence in your leadership.

Must be brave and accept the risk associated with a decision. Have courage. It builds character on your team.

Must have a competitive spirit but be a gracious loser. Always act in a professional manner, respecting others for their contributions. You will not always win, but you never give up. On to the next opportunity.

Must have endurance mentally and physically. A tired mind and a body without sustaining energy is a recipe for failure. Make sure that you exercise, get adequate rest, and keep your mind challenged.

Must listen to others. Control your ego and realize that others on your team will make mistakes. Figure out how to avoid the mistakes of the past and collectively come up with solutions. Defending the team at times is required so you don't make a decision that could negatively impact the direction and desired outcome of the team.

Must exercise extreme ownership in every decision made.

> *Leadership requires two things: a vision of the world that does not exist yet and the ability to communicate it.*
> —Simon Sinek

6

SUSTAINING TRANSFORMATIONAL LEADERSHIP

Transformational leadership is a calling, much more than a title. A transformational leader does not care about how he is called. He only cares about what he has been called to do.
—Gift Gugu Mona, *The Effective Leadership Prototype for a Modern-Day Leader*

Sustaining Leadership

One of the greatest gifts a leader can give an organization is the creation of a leadership legacy that sustains beyond their tenure. This includes continuously developing competencies, developing a leadership pipeline for aspiring leaders, creating core competencies, providing succession, and building a values culture that will be embraced by all in the organization.

Remember, people stay or leave because of leadership. Talented, energetic, and creative people want to work for a well-led organization that provides growth and the opportunity to create shared values. It also gives the organization a leg up in attracting and retaining the best and the brightest.

I have found that the key to sustained leadership is when you task yourself to not just create followers but rather develop those who you have responsibility for as leaders also. In so doing, you strengthen the organization, develop specialized competencies under your leadership, and create a culture where everyone is a leader. The energy level and commitment of each person in the organization is heightened, and the results gained are usually more than the desired result! You create a self-renewing culture of commitment and engagement that drives results. Leaders must have a genuine interest and desire to develop and strengthen the capacity of those they lead.

Here are some key points to consider:

1. *Self-refection is necessary.* Do you understand your own thinking, capabilities, styles, and skills as well as relating to those around you in your work environment? It is necessary to continuously be brutally honest with yourself about how you relate to others. Do they sense that you really care about their development and not just the attainment of a goal or assigned task? You must connect with your team consistently.

2. *Understand those you lead.* Employees are not all the same. You must leverage the unique talents and abilities of everyone. Understand them, their needs, ambitions, desires, and preferred work style. They have a need to know that you

know them and are there in their best interest. Give them a reason to want to lead with you!

3. *Develop skills and abilities.* Make sure that, as a leader, you are shoring up your own weak areas through continuous learning and development. Participation in a mastermind group is an option. This will enable you to share knowledge as well as provide training opportunities for others. Herein is an opportunity to develop soft skills, effective communication skills, analytic and strategic thinking, team facilitation and people-management capabilities. Additional focus may be appropriate as you initiate remote work and hybrid work environments to facilitate virtual team meetings.

4. *Apply your leadership skills and abilities.* Share and grow. Shared experiences bring about a deeper, richer learning experience. In many instances, you need to bridge the gap between intellectual, knowledge-based learning and applied, real-world competency development. Effective leaders find opportunities to put their learning into practice by serving those they lead. Share the knowledge and your experiences.

5. *Value feedback.* Feedback loops provide constructive feedback. They help us understand ourselves and our impact on those we lead and what their perceptions are. This is an area many individuals and companies fail to focus on. It is so essential to sustaining leadership within the organization. Formal 360 evaluations help leaders maximize their leadership over time. They provide valuable feedback loops that identify areas of needed focus as well as validation of positive leadership qualities within the organization. In your own self-evaluation, you learn from your successes and failures.

The more you are aware, the more you will care and invest in those you lead.

a. A useful resource for evaluating 360-degree evaluation software for your organization is at www.capterra.com.

b. The 360-degree evaluation software facilitates the feedback process between employees. This helps HR departments gather comprehensive information about the company's workforce, which can be used for both training and assessments purposes. Unlike performance assessment software, 360-degree feedback systems allow for the collection of information not only from superiors but peers, subordinates, and clients as well.

c. Benefits of 360-degree feedback:
   - reward top performers
   - identify blind spots
   - reduce the risk of discrimination

6. *Manage change.* Resilient leaders should boldly address difficult situations, such as business closures, layoffs, and furloughs rather than deflecting them and hoping no one will notice. Punit Renjen, CEO of Deloitte Global, stated, "Resilient leaders should decide and implement courses of action, even when unpopular. They should speak the truth about a situation, explain their decisions, and acknowledge the implications. Most importantly, they should listen to their people, even if what they hear is uncomfortable. In so doing, they can not only support their people but make better decisions by being greater grounded. Resilient leaders

can sustain their people, organizations, and society only if they sustain themselves."

Managing in a crisis prompts organizations to transform themselves to meet the challenges they will face. Whether it is changing market conditions, viral pandemics, changing financial markets, or consumer product/service changing preferences. Teams within organizations need to be more cross functional—not operating in silos. Teams must share best practices, ideas, experiences, resources, and technical expertise. Focus should be on the organization's strategic priorities. The Fortune/Deloitte CEO survey in 2020 found that CEOs' highest strategic priorities today stem from lasting changes in consumer behavior and customer engagement (70 percent), technologies or tools that will become part of "business as usual" (61 percent), and new or emerging business models (45 percent) that will sustain and improve performance.

Mr. Eenjen further states in his article "Resilient Leadership: Sustaining for the Long Haul," published August 25, 2020: "Resilient leaders can sustain their people, organizations, and communities only if they sustain themselves. They should be fit in mind, body, and purpose to continue to serve those constituencies while facing some of the most extraordinary challenges of their lifetimes, personal and professional. In times of stress, it is easy to revert to old, less effective approaches to leadership. Honest introspection and personal vulnerability can be key. To lead outwardly, we should first look inward."

Barbara Heller, in her article "Sustaining Leadership Greatness," May 1, 2017, addressed the importance of leadership competency in managing change:

The American Productivity and Quality Center completed a study about the effectiveness of change management in organizations and identified four important aspects of managing change for best practice agencies:

- Commitment to change from the very highest levels of the organization
- Alignment to the core strategy
- A strong model or methodology to guide the journey
- The ability to effectively and efficiently communicate the strategic message of change and a change in culture

The element that typically is missing from change management is the use of a strong model or methodology. The development of a framework assists with the organizations ability to develop change management as a core organizational competency. Here is a suggested checklist of actions which should be followed during a major change initiative:

- Are the purpose, direction and approach defined and documented clearly?
- Is the purpose understood by employees?
- Have you engaged individual or employee groups who can influence the outcome?
- Have you acknowledged their input and ideas?
- Are the necessary financial, human, technical resources in place?
- Is a strong and effective team ready to lead and guide the process?

- Do systems and processes support the change?
- Are leaders at all levels of the organization involved and committed?
- Do those affected by change have access to information and a way of providing ongoing input and feedback?
- Are systems in place to assess progress?

Effective communication is always required throughout the entire process. To many times, leadership assumes that everyone in the originations fully understands why the changes are being made and the resulting benefits to the business and them personally. That is a false assumption in many cases. Constant communication and internal focus groups will lend go a greater understanding and acceptance of the changes.

Closely related to change management is the ability to continuously innovate service delivery processes based on changing customer requirements and industry trends. Change is a constant in any organization, be prepared to plan and execute your strategy and be flexible to adjust in the process. Sustained leadership is not an option, but a critical element in changes made in any organization.

It is when we have an unwavering commitment to continually learning and developing others around us that we can lead great organizations, comprised of truly remarkable people, all contributing at their peak capacity. Leaders lead and create leaders in return.

Self-Discipline

*Respect your efforts, respect yourself. Self-respect leads to self-discipline.
When you have both firmly under your belt, that's real power.*
—Clint Eastwood

Ever start a project or specific task to improve your skills or maintain your level of successful achievement, and suddenly you catch yourself getting off track? For some reason, there is always a resistance that sways you away from being disciplined.

There are strategies that can help you become more self-disciplined, such as setting priorities, creating a set of strict rules that you manage your life by, and seeking and acknowledging external motivators. Sometimes the external motivators are the most effective (i.e., getting out of debt, learning new skills that will enable you to create wealth, seeking professional help to improve your relationships, or a specific search for a new career opportunity). Ready to be extremely honest with yourself? There are actions you can take or people who can influence you in being more disciplined in specific areas of your life. What would they be? List them below.

1. _____

2. _____

3. _____

4. _____

5. _____

Often, self-discipline is the combination of motivation, will power, and other mental traits. When we make mental shifts, things begin to happen. Remember, your biggest asset is changing the way you think and approach opportunities.

Motivation versus Habits

Most people seek what first motivates them when they want to get disciplined. Motivation alone is not the solution. It is how you approach the work to make the change. When the work starts, the motivation has a tendency to wane. Is it too hard? Is the pain of the work/task worth what you will gain?

Where is your focus? If it's motivation, it may dissipate over time. But if you focus on the work, you begin to develop habits that become routines. Those new routines lead to the accomplishment of the change at hand:

Examples:

If you want to lose weight, do not work out when you have spare time. Obesity accounts for 42 percent of the population, so it is a major problem that needs to be addressed. Is that you? Set a routine to work out three or four times a week. Make that your plan of attack to shed the pounds. It is a disciplined new routine to improve your physical well-being. To help with your motivation, secure the services of a personal trainer to jump-start your fitness program. Benefits include increasing your energy level, more mental alertness, and increased self-esteem. Secondly, aligned with the workouts, take a strong look at what you are eating and in what portions. Adjustments and discipline need to occur here as well. See a licensed dietician to get a plan in place. You win.

Do you want to build wealth so you can retire comfortably? Do not save your money just to buy things or use credit extensively, which only increases your debt load. What you need then is a plan to systematically set aside a set amount of money every month in investments that will work for you. Seek the guidance of a CERTIFIED FINANCIAL PLANNER™ professional CFP® who can help you with that plan. Once you begin that disciplined process, do not touch the money. Let it work for you.

Do you want to make a career shift? What additional degree and/or certifications will help you make that happen? Do your due diligence, use the tools that are in this book, and then chart your course of action—your plan!

- If it is a new degree, enroll in a college or university or technical institute and begin the process. Once you begin, discipline yourself to take courses every semester or quarter until you achieve your degree. Never skip a semester or quarter. Discipline yourself to go the course to completion.
- If you are going for certifications, take the necessary courses and study materials, take the necessary test, and get your certifications.
- If you are a professional, keep up with your continuing education credits (CEUs) so you maintain your professional standing.

As you go through a disciplined process, visualization is a good technique. Visualize yourself doing the work and accomplishing what you desire. See yourself accomplishing your planned objective.

Emotional versus Logical

Not to get technical or medically correct, but you have two brains that correspond to how you respond to circumstances and thought processes. The emotional side of your brain stimulates actions based on how you feel. The logical side helps you think clearly. You analyze objectively and logically how you are going to respond. Which one do you think will enable you to be more disciplined?

The answer is obvious—the logical!

What usually happens initially is an emotional response. The key is acknowledging that fact and moving from the emotional to the logical/rational approach to make good decisions.

Examples:

- *You want to write a book, right?* Do you begin to question if it is the right time to begin? Do you have enough experience and energy to begin? You question your ability to start. Your emotions of doubt play havoc with your emotional mind. What do you do? Stop, acknowledge how you are feeling emotionally, then sit down and begin to write your book. You can edit your work later in draft form. Remember, you can never have an ending to a task, such as authoring a book, until you begin the process!

- *You are not to snack between meals because you are on a diet.* Instead of going through endless mental debates in your head about whether you should or should not eat snacks between meals, you acknowledge your emotional desire to snack and allow your rational/logical thought process to surface the damage such a decision will result in, and you say no!

- *You are responsible for leading a team in completing a significant project that will benefit the company and your career.* You wrestle with allocating the required time to achieve the task with your team. Other pressing events in the company, which are more attractive, sidetrack you, and you feel conflicted. Your rational/logical side kicks in, and you weigh the benefits of completing the project. You set out to document your plan of action, schedule team meetings, make assignments, and proceed to complete the task.

- *You know that to get ahead in your profession, you need to have another degree as well a professional certification.* You are fearful of the time, expense, and commitment it will take to accomplish this goal. You are torn, and yet you realize that you will not advance in your career without taking this action. So you develop you plan, make provisions for the financial commitment, select your course plan, and begin the process. Once you start the process, you do not stop until it is completed. You will have demands for your time to get you off track from time to time, but you must say no to those occasions so you stay on track.

- *Ready for a job search?* But you are afraid to make a change. You are frustrated because you are not recognized for your accomplishments or compensated as you feel you are worth. You have dreams and desire to do more with your family and to build wealth for retirement. So you update your résumé and begin your search. It gets frustrating since you are not getting interviews, and then you stop your search out of frustration, and your emotional side kicks in. You settle for your current position, even though you are not fulfilled in your career—but you have a job! The mistake you made is you stopped the process! Remember, the moment you stop the process, you lose the opportunity. Someone else is always in the market for the very same career opportunity you are qualified for and they get the interview opportunity. Once you start your search, *do not stop*! It may take a long time before you get interviews, but it will happen at some point. You must continue your active search until the opportunities surface.

The key word here is *acknowledge*. In every instance, you need to move from the emotional side by acknowledging your feelings, be honest with yourself, and default your thought process to the logic/rational self. You should not depend on your emotions to keep you disciplined. Overreaching emotions create resistance, resulting in excuses to distract you.

You cannot control how you feel at any moment, but you can choose how you respond to your emotional triggers. Instead of letting your emotions control your decision-making process, acknowledge them, examine all the facts, options, and approaches, and then make the right choice by using your logical/rational brain.

Overoptimization

Optimization means to make things easier and to get them done as fast as possible with the least effort possible. Overoptimization leads us to dwell on the small stuff that does not have any impact on what we are trying to accomplish. The goal of making things simpler and easier is not about less. It is about eliminating the nonessential things so you can focus on the things that matter.

If you want to improve your life, you intentionally optimize—make it harder! When you play a sport, having an opponent who is better than you can challenge and improve your game. Why? Because you play harder to win, and in the challenge, you observe the tactics used by your opponent. You learn and intensely compete to win and improve your game.

Pushing your limits incrementally does not just help you get better at what you want to do; it also makes the base-level habits and routines easier and less difficult.

In Summary

1. Focus on building habits that result in healthy routines rather than depending on motivation.
2. Act with a thoughtful and determined mindset rather than approaching every action based on emotions.
3. Stop optimizing to make things easier; instead, make things more challenging for growth.

Critical Thinking

Responsibility to yourself means refusing to let others do your thinking, talking, and naming for you; it means learning to respect and use your own brains and instincts; hence, grappling with hard work.
— Adrienne Rich

One of the most important skills is the ability to think critically. It is the ability to think rationally and put together logical connections. It is self-guided and self-disciplined thinking. In 2020, a report by the World Economic Forum confirmed that senior executives around the world view critical thinking skills as essential, and they expect these skills to be increasingly important for workplace success.

In a recent survey by Dale Carnegie Training across twenty countries and territories, 57 percent of respondents identified critical thinking as among the top skills needed to prepare to be successful to work in an environment complemented by artificial intelligence, ranking it tied with teamwork and behind only communication skills and creativity. (Dale Carnegie White Paper: *Critical Thinking: The Essential Skill for Navigating the Future*, Dale Carnegie.com).

From time to time, you have used critical thinking as a process to solve critical problems and create new opportunities for you personally as well as your company. Here are some steps to consider:

1. *Access and evaluate your resources of information.* Assemble as much information as you can. Utilize creative, innovative concepts and pros and cons of various approaches to your decision-making process. When you come across an idea, memorialize it; write it down and save it. Some of the greatest ideas come in a passing moment, and you must record it before you forget it. Retain all your resources so you can access in the future as the occasion arises.

2. *Seek out good thinkers.* Aside from gaining insight through books, articles, and white papers, seek out influencers who are valuable resources to share as well as challenge your thinking process. One resource we have addressed in this book is mastermind groups.

3. *Focus.* Be intentional about what you are thinking. Be serious with yourself. Focus on the positive outcomes of your decision. There is no room for negative thoughts, which usually result in adverse outcomes.

4. *Take action.* It is not just enough to simply think good thoughts. Act on them. Some thoughts that result in actions have a truly short shelf life, so you must act on them. Sometimes time is of the essence, and if you fail to act, you will miss the opportunity to get the results you desire.

5. *Create continued momentum.* Use critical thinking to continue to generate more great ideas. Allow yourself to practice visualization. Seeing what could be creates an atmosphere of creativity that is energized by critical thinking.

Everyone thinks. It is our nature to do so. But so much of our thinking, left to itself, is biased, distorted, partial, uninformed, or downright prejudiced. Yet the quality of our life and that of what we produce, make, or build depends precisely on the quality of our thoughts. Shoddy thinking is costly, both in money and quality of life. Excellence in thought, however, must be systematically cultivated.

A well-cultivated thinker:

- raises vital questions and problems, formulating them clearly and precisely
- gathers and assesses relevant information, using abstract ideas to interpret it
- effectively comes to well-reasoned conclusions and solutions, evaluating them against relevant critical standards

- thinks open-mindedly within alternative systems of thought, recognizing and assessing, as need be, their assumptions, implications, and practical consequences
- communicates effectively with others in figuring out solutions to complex problems

Critical thinking is, in short, self-directed, self-disciplined, self-monitored, and self-corrective thinking. Critical thinking results in living with a purpose, based on a critical assessment of all the options in the decision-making process. Making a concerted effort to stop the "react and respond" behavior and purposefully changing your direction to think critically is required for you to live a life with a purpose and a plan.

Critical thinking is a skill you attain, developing your judgments by thinking open-mindedly, logically, and coherently. You become a more independent and self-directed learner. Every person can improve their critical thinking skills.

Here is why practicing critical thinking enriches your life:

Independent thinking is powerful. You do not rely on others, and you take complete ownership of your strengths and weaknesses. This helps you to avoid mistakes, improving your judgment and evaluation skills.

Your mere presence and presentation skills are enhanced. By critical thinking, you can present your thoughts in an organized manner. Your ideas and how you communicate with others are much more effective.

Who does not like making good decisions? A good systematic and logical thinker can coherently outline workable solutions to problems. In this process, you also utilize visualization so you can mentally see the outcome of your decision.

How do you see yourself and your communication with others? Critical thinking improves your self-evaluation. Thinking and reasoning helps you reflect on your values and decisions. It improves your self-esteem and well-being. As you see yourself in a positive light, others sense your energy and purpose when you communicate with them individually, as do groups when you make a presentation.

Keeping up to date is important. Are you relevant in the present moment? Since our economy and technology are ever changing, digesting the latest information helps us adapt to our ever-changing world. You must continually evaluate new concepts, ideas, and technology in a critical thought process to make decisions that correlate to the present culture and the evolution of the workplace.

There are three types of thinkers:

Selfish thinkers. You are smart, but you do not care about others. You could be narcissistic in your approach to life, and your focus is your own self-interest. Frequently you manipulate other people to get what you want, not always for the common good. People get hurt in the process, but you do not care. There is negative energy in thinking selfishly; however, if this same intensity of energy were redirected in a positive light, everyone would benefit.

Naive thinkers. You believe everything you hear. You do not ask questions, and you go along with whatever your friends, colleagues, or the media communicates to you. You do not evaluate to see if there is evidence of fact to support what you are hearing. We refer to this as herd mentality. You just go along with the current trend or thought within a group/organization, and whatever the group decides, you go along with. You rely on other people to do the thinking for you. The outcomes are not always positive.

Fair-minded thinkers. You do not believe everything you hear. You are smart and empathetic. You love to evaluate what you hear by asking questions, searching for verification of facts on the internet and other sources. You collaborate with think tanks, mentors, and/ or mastermind groups to make the best-informed decisions in your personal and professional lives. Such thinkers have the potential to become great, wise critical thinkers who will have influence in this world.

Our role in society should always be to develop more fair-minded thinkers. In so doing, we will be bringing up future successful decisions makers for the good of all society. Give critical thought to how you approach your thought process. If you are other than a fair-minded thinker, now is the time to adjust.

The following stages of developing critical thinking will help:

Knowledge. Make it a practice to begin to acquire new knowledge. Educate yourself on the environment around you. Use the internet, listen to competing media sources and viewpoints, and do your own research. Reading books always helps us understand our country's history; even reading historical novels sometimes brings history into greater understanding. Do your own research. Apply the scientific method to theories you are presented to evaluate their validity and application. Check for credibility. When the opinion and research come to an understandable conclusion, you have arrived at a new updated knowledge bank that you can draw from when making decisions. Always keep in mind that life is a continuum, and everything changes over time—so keep up to date!

Comprehension. Take what you have learned in the knowledge phase and relate it to your present knowledge. To comprehend is to apply the research you have done in point one to update your knowledge bank and enhance your ability to comprehend new concepts and principles from which you can benefit. You are complementing what you know with new information, expanding your knowledge base.

Application. Now that you have gained knowledge and comprehend what you have learned, it is time to apply the results of your critical thought process. Think through clearly what you have learned in this process and visualize how new insights and information will improve the quality of your life. This can apply to your professional life as well (i.e., completion of an assigned project, professional goal, or team objective).

In making business project decisions, you must analyze the data collected. Does the data align with your critical and logical thinking, and is it relevant to the project or goal you are seeking to accomplish? Is it relevant? If so, then the data has true application to arrive at the desired result.

By interpreting and evaluating the data you have already analyzed and synthesized, you can draw a reasonable conclusion resulting in the desired outcome. You have guarded your emotional side. When you let your emotions take over, you may push your evaluation back, and you will not make progress. The fact is, if you have taken the time and done your critical thinking as suggested in this book, you are more likely ready to act and make your decision. It is time to press on!

Mastering excellence in critical thinking is the key. The important thing is to be smarter and not work harder. Know your strengths and weaknesses. Believe in the voice of reason and logic, and you will solve problems and create new opportunities in a healthy and efficient way.

Common Mistakes to Avoid

1. Your comfort zone is your worst enemy. Our subconscious minds tend to look for information that confirms what we already know. In this case, we do not question our beliefs or thought process on a given topic or situation. Instead of looking for differences, we feel safer just staying the way we are. Status quo is safe.

2. Our minds naturally tend to cause us to worry about our losses rather than focusing on our gains in life. If a change is going to cost us in time and money, we worry about how much it will cost—period. We become paralyzed and do not move forward. Many times, the cost is well worth the reward we will experience. The outcome is incredibly positive, and we take pride in the achievement we have made.

3. Incorrect predictions are the result of our emotions taking control, and we make wrong decisions. When our emotions rule, the outcome is not thought out clearly, and we just settle for the outcome—whether good or bad. We become indifferent.

4. You realize you have made the wrong decision, but your mind tricks you into believing that it was the right thing to do, to make it feel better! Our emotions again become our worst enemy.

5. Facts are important. However, sometimes our minds mislead us to believe something is better just by comparing it to something else. It might not be the right decision, but now it is the more attractive choice.

Groupthink Bias—Herd Mentality

Research has proven that most humans value social conformity so much that they'll change their own responses—even their perceptions-to align with the group, even when the group is blatantly wrong.
—Bill Blalock

Groupthink is when individuals tend to refrain from expressing doubts and judgments or disagreeing with the consensus. In the interest of making a decision that furthers their group cause, members may also ignore ethical or moral consequences. While it is often invoked at the level of geopolitics or within business organizations, it can also be applicable in subtle processes, such as rationalizing a poor decision being made by one's friends.

Decades of research show people tend to go along with the majority view, even if that view is objectively incorrect. The two leading theories of conformity are that people look to a group because they are unsure of what to do, and people go along with the norm because they are afraid of being different, said Dr. George Berns, professor of psychiatry and behavioral sciences at Emory University School of Medicine in Atlanta, Georgia. Bern's research, which he describes in the book *Iconoclast: A Neuroscientist Reveals How to Think Differently*, found that brain mechanisms associated with fear and anxiety do play a part in situations where a person feels his or her opinion goes against the grain.

Examples of Groupthink—Herd Mentality

- *Investing.* Instead of making independent decisions, you make decisions based on emotions and instinct. Many times, investors make rash, on-the-spot decisions based on what their friends are doing. The quick decisions are made without any insight into the risk associated with the investment. People make rash decisions because they are fearful of embarrassment with their friends or being wrong. The fear of being wrong always goes against your better judgment in making better choices that are more logical and researched. Some investment firms have been known to approach their clients to buy a certain stock because they are part of the underwriting, and they have stock to unload on their clients, so they fulfill their commitment to the company being listed. This is often true with initial public offerings (IPOs). Always be on guard when being approached to make a quick decision on your investments. Prudent investments have a higher probability of working to your benefit in the long run. Beware!
- *Social groups.* People tend to gravitate to larger influential groups or groups that are popular based on social class, profession, or political affiliation. Ever hear of peer pressure? That term is more often used when young people are in school. That is when we begin the process of familiar association with others that gives us identity and status. It carries through to adulthood. Sometimes those group associations

compromise your personal and professional values. Pay close attention to who you associate yourself with. Over time, your identity becomes a reflection of the social groups you are a part of. It works both ways—positive and negative! So be on guard and choose well.

- *Beliefs/spirituality.* Your belief system is the core of who you are. A following sometimes develops into a community. Not entirely like a cult but similar. A person's belief can quickly become a community's belief. The bigger the community, the larger the influence of others to join. This is very evident in what religion you practice and what form of worship and values you are taught. Be careful. Do your own research and decide what you truly believe in. Then find a faith that aligns with your spiritual beliefs and convictions.

The aforementioned examples are very real to all of us. However, a word of caution is embedded in each of these examples. As a result, it may be safer to avoid such associations.

Groupthink / herd mentality can be mentally unhealthy. If you have a huge group of people of subpar intelligence, and you add a few highly intelligent people to the large group, do you think the group will become smarter? The answer is a resounding no.

The intelligence level of the group does not change when a different form of stimulus joins in. It's usually the opposite. Most of the time, if intelligent people decide to join such a group, their higher intelligence is dormant to the group or ignored. People have a strong desire to fit in and be a part of a group. We suppress our intelligence so we do not appear to be smarter than others or to think more highly of ourselves than the group. When you know people in a particular group, you tend to conform to the norm of the group. Beware!

Instead of conforming to the norm, stop taking the easy route and agreeing with people just because they work with you or are a part of your family. They could even be your friends. By conforming to the norm, you are not seeking your own identity. Going against the grain is hard, but you must choose conflict at times to divorce yourself from the social herd mentality norm.

Know who you are. Spend time with yourself. Find out what makes you happy without any influence of another human being. You can learn from others as you question your identity. Do not let the group define you. Know who you are and what you stand for.

Here are five strategies to decrease the likelihood that you will simply defer to the social default when making choices:

1. *Take time to make decisions.* Do not rush. Take time to make decisions by asking questions and thinking about your options. Others may feel uncomfortable because they want you to hurry up and decide. Just because everyone else seems to be making a quick decision does not mean they know best.

2. *Do not be on autopilot.* When you do not stop and take time to consider your options, you go through the motions as if you are on autopilot. Instead of doing our own due diligence, we see what others are doing, and we simply copy. When you are aware that you have this tendency, you can begin to make conscious decisions for yourself that are in your best interest.

3. *Be the exception.* Many times, we social default to the group to feel accepted. When you do, you settle for less. Successful

people do not always excel by sticking with the group. Instead, they stand out and dare to explore, challenge those around them, and do things differently. To be successful, you need to be exceptional and not the norm. Do not allow people to tell you what you should think, feel, or do. Take time to evaluate whether the choices you are making are really yours.

4. *Form your own opinion.* Make a conscious effort, with facts in hand, to act on your terms. Develop your own opinion. Rather than adopt the herd mentality, educate yourself about your choices so you can make a well-informed decision.

5. *Be aware of your stress level.* If you are stressed about something going on in your personal life or distracted by another significant event around you, you are at a greater risk of following the herd. Recognize that risk and put off making a quick decision until you can concentrate on the task at hand. Stress can be an extraordinarily strong distraction in making well-informed decisions.

Another common tendency is to rely too heavily, or *anchor*, on one trait or piece of information when making a decision. This is commonly referred to as anchoring. During normal decision making, individuals anchor, or overly rely, on specific information or a specific value and then adjust to that value to account for other elements of the circumstance. Once the anchor is set, there is a bias toward that value. That bias can prove to be very costly and thus should be carefully evaluated before making the final decision. Is there a better course of action? Are you utilizing analytics to fully understand the strategy being considered? Will you achieve the desired outcome you seek?

Extreme Ownership

*On any team, in any organization, all responsibility for success
and failure rests with the leader. The leader must own everything
in his or her world. There is no one else to blame.*
—Extreme Ownership

The success of any organization rests with leaders who own their decisions. You must acknowledge your mistakes and admit failures, take ownership of them, and develop a plan to win.

Jocko Willink and Leif Babin, in their book *Extreme Ownership* (St. Martin's Press, NYC, 2015, 2017), stated, "the direct responsibility of a leader includes getting people to listen, support and execute plans. You can't *make* people listen to you. You can't *make* them execute. But to implement real change, to drive people to accomplish something truly complex or difficult or dangerous—you can't *make* people do those things. You have to *lead* them."

To lead, you have to fully understand the task at hand, why you are doing this task/project and what the desired outcome is. If you as a leader do not understand the why of the task/project, how can you expect others to believe and follow you? Ask questions until you understand the why so you can believe in what you are doing, and you can pass that information down to your team with confidence so they can get out and execute. That is leadership.

Extreme ownership requires leaders to look at an organization's problems through the objective lenses of reality, without emotional attachments to agendas or plans. It mandates that a leader set ego aside, accept responsibility for failures, attack weaknesses, and consistently work to build a better and more effective team and company.

Leadership is not about power. It is about leading people to levels of great achievement. It is about empowering and inspiring people to rise up to be their best. Then it's a win for everyone.

Leadership has nothing to do with having power over someone; it's about using your influence to inspire and empower your people to achieve the impossible.

You can have a team that is comprised of extremely talented players in sports, or have direct reports in a company, or a leadership team that is highly skilled with advanced degrees and a history of past accomplishments, and they can fail quickly if they are not led properly. It's been proven many times that you can take a group that has been subpar, replace management with true leaders who own their decisions, and see the rebirth of a winning team. Leaders must lead in order to achieve greatness. Seek to lead, and you will achieve greatness.

Being an Advocate

I've learned that people will forget what you said, people will forget what you did, but people will never forget how you made them feel.
—Maya Angelou

We don't want to push our ideas on to customers, we simply want to make what they want.
—Laura Ashley

Service, in short, is not what you do, but who you are. It's a way of living that you need to bring to everything you do if you're to bring it to your customer interactions.
—Betsy Sanders

*Happy customers are your biggest advocates and
can become your most successful sales team.*
—Lisa Masiello

Design experiences that are emotionally resonant with your client/customer so that they feel better about your interaction with them and remember it. In so doing, you facilitate positive emotions for a positive outcome.

It is human nature that people like to be in control of their lives and what is going on around them. Uncertainty creates anxiety. So be specific about what value you bring to your client/customer. Be specific!

Be an advocate for your client/customer. The experience is as valuable as the product or service that you are offering. It is not about you. Consider what your customer cares about. Get into their shoes and see things from their perspective. Keep them well informed, and when there is a problem or concern expressed, listen carefully, be transparent, and address the concern head-on and find a solution. No excuses. Own it.

Jon Picoult, in his recent book, *From Impressed to OBSESSED—12 Principals for Turning Customers and Employees into Lifelong Fans* (McGraw Hill Publishing, 2022), Mr. Picoult gives some great insight into customer/client relationship. Here are a few principles to consider:

- "Embrace a Velcro approach to customer service. Here's what advocacy-amplifying ownership looks like: Imagine going to work every day dressed in a Velcro suit. Now imagine that every customer request or inquiry is like a Velcro ball thrown at you. It sticks like glue. In practice, which means assuming exceptional ownership and accountability for every customer request that lands in your lap. And if you have to farm out the request to coworkers for assistance, you always keep a string on it, following up with your colleagues [and the customer] to make sure the request is handled properly."

- On many occasions, it may require a resolution at a team level. "The alternative is to use a tightly knit group, cross functional teams comprised of employees with complimentary expertise."

- "Use solution-orientated language. Rather than telling customers what you can't do, focus on telling them what you can do. This is especially important when the customer is dissatisfied for some reason and is seeking resolution to a problem. Instead of pointing to policy, procedure, or system constraints to explain why you can't do something, assume a solution-orientated posture, using such phrases as 'Let's figure out what we can do here to help you.' Those words alone won't turn the customer into a raving fan, but by implying advocacy, they can help de-escalate difficult situations."

Do not force your client/customer to make a decision based on your own desires. Your client/customer is the decision maker. Through focus groups, surveys, product sampling, and the power of analytics, you will gain insight into what products and services you should offer and support. Then you will strengthen the relationship. They will perceive that you really know their business and that what you are offering has true value to them and their company and/or customers.

If you are part of an organization, club, or a professional association where committees are in place to address upstream the concerns of members and their concerns, listen and talk less. Be an advocate for the membership and take to heart their suggestions and input to work toward solutions to improve the member experience. Do not just send someone else to the meetings; show up and bring with you resources that can provide input for an improved member experience. Do not be reactive or passive in committee meetings. You and your committee members are advocates for the membership to find solutions and create memorable moments and great experiences. Own it!

Never forget that you are to be an advocate for your client/customer and any organization in which you collaborate with committees. You will have greater credibility. They will perceive you as being transparent and open to addressing their concerns, as well as believing in the product or services you provide and enhancing the member experience.

Being an advocate is a great reflection of true leadership!

Team Building

Teamwork is the ability to work together toward a common vision. The ability to direct individual accomplishments toward organizational objectives. It is the fuel that allows common people to attain uncommon results.
—Andrew Carnegie, industrialist, and philanthropist

*Coming together is a beginning. Keeping together
is progress. Working together is success.*
—Henry Ford, industrialist

As a result of the COVID pandemic, the workplace has made a paradigm shift. For many, remote work is now the norm. For others, there is the advent of the four-day work week or hybrid approach (remote and in the office). For work to be accomplished, we look at work based on time, task, or both. With this shift in mind, team building is critical.

Leading Virtual, Hybrid, and In-House Corporate Leadership Teams

Be the trusted team leader!

Trust is a strong factor in having an effective virtual team. James M. Citrin and Darlene Derosa, in their book *Leading at a Distance—Practical Lessons for Virtual Success* (John Wiley & Sons, Inc., 2021), offer some practical insights in how to have an effective virtual team:

Trust is built naturally among teams that interact in person each day, but it takes more effort to develop among teams that rarely [if ever] meet face to face. Virtual leaders need to create an environment that fosters trust. When trust breaks down, however, they will struggle to be productive.

Trust is a prerequisite for virtual team success, but it's harder to build virtually: 39% of executives report experiencing challenges in building trust in a remote environment. Building task-based trust early on is important for virtual teams.

Leaders can create a trusting environment through open, frequent, and transparent communication; by encouraging team members to share aspects of their personal lives to build intimacy; and by admitting when they don't know something.

Signs of low virtual trust include poor communication, a culture of blame, unresolved conflicts, lack of follow through, silos, and an "I" orientation instead of a "we" orientation.

As a virtual team leader, it is essential that members on your team have the discipline to work independently in order to deliver on the tasks assigned. At the same time, each team member must work collaboratively with others on the team, providing continuous feedback on what is and is not working. They must share a common goal to complete the task as assigned. It is much more than just time accounted for. It is results delivered!

Help your virtual team find its *why* and then focus on the *how*.

Simon Sinek, a well-known motivational speaker and author of *New York Times* best-selling books, such as *Leaders Eat Last: Why Some Teams Pull Together and Others Don't*, talks at length about answering the question of why in his TED talks about inspiring others to action (*Start with Why* by Simon Sinek, Penguin Books, Ltd.):

Every single person, every single organization on the planet knows what they do, 100 percent. But very, very few people or organizations know why they do what they do. And by "why" I don't mean "to make a profit." That's a result. What's your cause? What's your belief? Why does your organization exist? Why do you get out of bed in the morning? And why should anyone care? As a result, the way we think, we act, the way we communicate is from the outside in, it's obvious. We go from the clearest thing to the fuzziest thing. But the inspired leaders and the inspired organizations—regardless of their size, regardless of their industry—all think, act and communicate from the inside out.

One aspect that separates truly inspirational leaders from their peers is the ability to understand and explain the "why" of their organization to others. Leaders start with answering "why" because, once their team understands that they know they aren't just driving profits so others can make money, they're making a difference in people's lives, in their industry, community and world at large.

Whether you are leading a virtual, hybrid, or in-house leadership team, the same principle applies to understand the why in order to know how to deliver on the assigned task or corporate objective.

Dana Harvey (www.danaharveycommunications.com), in her article "5 Vital Virtual Communication Skills," published March 27, 2020, clearly states, "The way we work, meet, network, and collaborate may never be the same after COVID-19." With a passion for emerging technologies, she is well versed on blockchain, AI, big data, next-generation wireless data, telecom infrastructure, and more.

Dana is a corporate communications professional with more than twenty-five years of global experience using strategic internal and external communications to launch products, build brands, develop teams, educate markets, and grow revenues.

The virus inadvertently turned in-office teams into virtual teams, heralded the influx of remote workers, pushed live events to be held online, and created opportunities for people to learn to build their business networks from the confines of their own homes.

I share with you her five vital virtual communication skills to stay effective, connected, and inspired:

Suddenly, virtual communication is the norm!

During this transition from face-to-face to online communication in the workplace, effective communication skills are more important than ever. Scientists say that only 7% of our communication is in the words we use—55% is body language and 38% is tone of voice. So sure, your teammates may be able to hear you on calls, chat with you over Slack, and see you on a videoconference, but all online communication methods miss out on some of the cues we take for granted. Even on a video call, your colleague can't see you tapping your foot impatiently waiting for you to hurry up and get to the point! They can't see you working away diligently at your desk or engrossed in a meeting in the conference room, and it's challenging to build rapport when you can't cross paths in the lunchroom or stop for a casual chat on your way to your desk.

There are a plethora of mediums and tools for online communication, and while they can be effective in bridging the gaps between us, it's up to us as individuals to build our communication skills in the era of the virtual workplace.

Focus on these 5 virtual communication skills to increase productivity and morale for yourself and your virtual teams:

1) Be respectful

Behind every avatar is a real person, so even if you are not seeing your colleagues or clients face-to-face, remember they deserve the same respect you would give them in person.

Failure to respect others' time and focus erodes trust and leads to disengagement and under-productivity.

Show up on-time: Just as you would not show up late to an in-person meeting, respect others' time by showing up on-time (or even be there waiting early) for online meetings. Make sure you have the video link handy, so you aren't scrambling around at the last minute trying to find it and make it easy for others by including video links directly in calendar invites you send.

Be professional and prepared: A virtual meeting is still a meeting. Show up looking, feeling, and sounding professional. Check yourself—do you need to take a shower? Put on a clean shirt? Move your computer to a place with a professional-looking background? Take a quick break to get your mind ready and focused prior to the meeting? Grab a coffee or water? Do what you need to do to have a professional mindset and appearance.

Focus: When your teammates can't actually see what you're doing, it's tempting to multitask during virtual meetings. Don't. Focus on the person or people and the topic at hand. Silence your phone, minimize your other screens, and—even if you're on mute or off video—don't eat, go to the bathroom, or walk away.

Don't interrupt: Don't derail purposeful threads or channels with off-topic conversations—just as you wouldn't interrupt an in-person meeting to talk about non-work-related issues.

2) Get to the point

Have you ever been on a call or video meeting where a speaker just went on and on until you tuned out? Without the in-person visual cues that let you know how the receivers of your message are taking it in, it can be easy to think you need to talk more or to just not clue in when you've already talked too much. Clarity and conciseness are basic, elemental communication skills that must be practiced for effective virtual communication. Clarity means expressing your point simply and directly, and conciseness means not wasting words. Remember, your colleagues are busy, too, so respect them by getting to the point.

3) Get personal

Even when working remotely, human beings are social creatures who crave a feeling of connection. Remote workers can feel isolated and disconnected, and the better we know our colleagues, the easier it is to work together. In fact, a recent Gallup study shows lack of social interaction with co-workers is a leading cause for remote workers' morale, engagement, and productivity to decline. Close-knit teams are proven to be more empathetic and more invested in seeing each member succeed, leading to better corporate resiliency and business results. So, in lieu of in-person "water cooler conversations," make time to get personal with your team: spend the first few minutes of a meeting asking what's going on in your colleagues' lives; get team members to share a personal highlight of their day; set up virtual coffee chats or "beer o'clock" to strengthen relationships and build rapport. Don't mistake taking the time to build relationships as a contradiction to "get to the point"—while you need to handle business issues concisely, you also need to build personal connections and create emotional bonds that will hold you together as a team in the face of challenges. Personally, I think whoever said "absence makes the heart grow fonder" never worked in a remote team!

4) Over-communicate

So many unscheduled conversations and clarifications take place when we physically work together, helping us stay both aligned and inspired. It's easy for remote workers to "disappear" if they don't proactively communicate and also for them to feel forgotten or isolated if they are not proactively communicated with. It's critical for virtual teams to over-communicate by asking questions, clarifying objectives, reporting progress on goals, encouraging and affirming others' efforts, stating requirements, and providing feedback. Be deliberate in your communications, keeping in mind you are all lacking the insights you would gain from non-verbal cues and casual conversations. Ask or tell if you need something, if you're waiting on something, what progress you are making, if you have extra time, or if you don't understand. Over-communicating will help avoid surprises, keep everyone on the same page, and ensure invisibility and isolation factors don't lead to diminished productivity.

5) Focus on the message received

Any communication—whether in person or virtual—has two components: message sent and message received. The most competent communicators direct their energy toward how their message is received, thus focusing more on the audience or other person and less on themselves. All communicators should do this when their message is virtual. With virtual communication lacking the subtle cues of in-person interaction, it's easy for messages to be misinterpreted or misunderstood. Emotions—love them or hate them—can help add emotion to messages sent digitally. Gifs can also help convey the right nuances. Be aware of strong language; use exclamation points with consideration; be careful with dry humor and sarcasm; never use all caps unless you are intending your message to come across as yelling; pause for feedback and questions if you are communicating by video or phone. Misconstrued messages can lead to resentment, confusion, frustration, and disengagement. A useful tip for written communication is to read everything out loud to yourself before you send it.

Bonus Tip: Be Forgiving

Remember, for many of us, working remotely is an unexpected and unwelcome necessity during a pandemic. Some people thrive working remotely, and for others, it is a struggle. Many of us have our kids home from school with us now, too, adding extra distractions. And on top of everything, many of us—even those who are accustomed to working from home—are dealing with new and uncomfortable challenges and emotions. Let's all cut each other a little slack and practice another vital soft skill that will help us survive this time both professionally and personally: empathy.

In Summary

Whether we were ready for it or not, whether we like it or not, COVID-19 has pushed more of us than ever into the realm of remote work and distributed teams. To stay effective and inspired, we need to hone our virtual communication skills. Virtual communication requires more thoughtfulness than in-person communication because we miss non-verbal cues, we don't have the opportunity for impromptu chats, and messages are more easily misconstrued. Try to be more deliberate with your virtual communication by focusing on these 5 vital skills. Why? Well, besides the human connectedness factor, according to a study by Watson Wyatt, companies whose employees communicate effectively, in general, have a 47% higher total return to shareholders and are four times more likely to report high levels of employee engagement. Communication is a soft skill that leads to hard business results, and in this COVID-19 world, virtual communication needs more focus than ever.

Even in a post COVID-19 environment, the transition to a virtual environment will continue to be an effective means of communication. The beauty of a virtual environment is that you are not confined to a physical office location, and you can effectively manage anywhere in the world. A paradigm shift in the workplace has happened, and it will never be the same again! Make sure you are a part of it!

Decisiveness

> *Indecisiveness is the number one reason for failure. Lack of ability to make a decision in a timely manner causes most people to fail with their projects and plans. Identify this challenge and decide to no longer let it be a setback from your success.*
> —Farshad Asl, *The "No Excuses" Mindset: A Life of Purpose, Passion, and Clarity*

Being Decisive

You have to make decisions! Decisiveness is defined as being characterized by firmness and making a decision. Being decisive means that you have the ability to decide. From the strength of a decision, you then have the ability to act. Leadership requires that you are able to make key decisions. Decisiveness simply means being the leader of your own life. Decisiveness is both a skill you can build and an internal state that you can summon when you need it.

Hasty decisions are not to be confused with being decisive. You act with speed and clarity. Indecisive people act that way simply because they feel others will make better decisions. These people end up being subjected to the whims of others and have to rely on the thinking power of others to survive. As a leader, you cannot be indecisive!

You observe the information you have available, and then you decide what would be the most efficient and successful course of action. If you have additional resources you can summon in the process, you gather that information and then decide with the facts available.

Unfortunately, most people procrastinate. People who have a propensity to avoid or delay making a decision usually don't make progress in their life or career.

There is an element of uncertainty at times, but the urgency of the moment demands that you proceed with the information you have available at that time. The best decision is the best one you can make with the information available at the time. Will you make mistakes at times? Of course, you will. But you went with the best available information at that moment, and time was of the essence. When mistakes happen, that's when extreme ownership comes into play as a leader. You review the gaps and where you were not successful, take corrective action, alter your plan, and move forward to your final solution. A decisive person will learn from each decision so that the next one has a larger base of information and is more likely to succeed.

Decisiveness is more than just a skill; it is an emotion. There must have been moments when you felt decisive. Certainly, it felt different then when you were confused and unsure. In those instances, you procrastinated. Decisiveness is similar to a feeling of confidence, strength, and assuredness. All are the by-products of successful leadership.

Recall a time when you felt particularly decisive. How did you feel? Did you find your posture with your head held high and your breathing calm? Your movements were deliberate, controlled, and smooth. Your voice resonated and was resolute. This physiology is characteristic of your feeling of being decisive. Also, others will notice your demeanor. They will see you as confident, and that feeling will resonate within your team, making them more assured and productive. Leadership demands decisive, well-informed actions that build confidence and respect.

Remember, indecisiveness is also a decision. The choice is yours.

Start to train your brain to approach decision-making a different way. You need to tell yourself:

- Decide to be decisive.
- Picture yourself as a decisive person. Use visualization.
- Stop worrying about bad decisions.
- Be brave in the face of mistakes.
- Seek facts and get back on track with a solution.

Don't wait for certainty before you make some decisions. Don't let others make decisions for you. Operate from an internal source of strength and confidence and plan the right course of action. Be decisive.

Overcoming Roadblocks

Honestly, I've found the best way to overcome roadblocks is to ask for help and with an open mind. Someone might have advice I can use, a connection that could bring new leads, or just the right word of understanding to help bolster my spirit as I persevere. My success as an entrepreneur has come in large part because kind, wise people heard my struggles and gave me the benefit of their experience.
—Andi Cumbo-Floyd

Roadblocks, only block the road if you stop and let them. Action, action, action! Roadblocks don't block you from going left, right, over or under. Assess your options, come up with more options, don't stop, stay focused on the actions you need to take on your journey. Keep true to your why, and you will find a way around.
—Mary Kathryn Johnson

Here is a situation you may relate to. You are progressing along in your career, and everything seems to be in order. You are making progress on your projected career path. You are feeling comfortable, and you are consistently meeting your objectives. You finish your most recent project, and suddenly something is preventing you from taking the next step—that next opportunity.

Overcoming roadblocks in your career is inevitable. It happens to everyone at some point. No matter what point you are at in your career, you are bound to face hurdles. Some of them can set you back, halt your progress, or even derail your plans. Some challenges cause you to question your abilities. You might be dealing with an excessive workload, conflicts with colleagues, change in company management and culture, lack of motivation, or being stuck in a role that does not match your skills.

The key to a solution is the word *hurdle*. We tend to look at roadblocks as an end, no way around, full stop. Not the case. We have to hurdle the challenge just like an Olympic athlete takes on the hurdles in a race. It's time to move with determination and speed to overcome what you are facing.

Whatever obstacles you are facing in your career, look at them as part of your path to growth and sustained success. There are valuable lessons to be learned. Overcoming your roadblock can take your skills to the next level. With your success of overcoming, you will have a better vision of yourself and what your next steps are as you continue your career journey.

Here are some tips to help you break down barriers and overcome the roadblocks in your life:

1. *Avoid fear.* This is a natural emotion we all experience from time to time—more intensely when it comes to our careers. Fear is a normal part of life. But you need to overcome fear with courage in order to resolve your situation. Don't let fear get in your way. You need to stop, reflect, and come up with logical solutions. Think about how you will feel emotionally once you overcome the situation, rather than dwelling on the fear of what you are facing. Will you feel relieved, fulfilled, respected? Try to focus on that positive feeling and let it drown out your fear. The only way you learn and grow is facing the roadblock head-on and going through it for a positive outcome.

2. *View your situation as an opportunity.* Remember, you cannot always control the circumstances around you, but you can always control how you react to them. Your brain is very elastic, and you can change your pattern of thoughts. The brain is a physical organ, whereas the mind is more a collection of thoughts, emotions, imaginations, and memories. When compared to a computer, the brain acts as the hardware, while the mind is the software within it, and you can upgrade or reprogram your mind for success in different ways.

3. *Your subconscious mind is the key.* The subconscious mind refers to the information that is accessible when you need it. It can also work against you. Instead of thinking in a positive direction to overcome the obstacles for a lasting change, we revert back to our old way of thinking—in our careers, our finances, our relationships, our health, and our general sense of well-being. In essence, we have sabotaged any potential for change and a successful direction in our lives.

So you need to shift your mindset in order to move forward.

1. Decide that you need to change your thinking. You need absolute clarity in what you want out of your life and career. What outcome do you seek? The more thought you put into this process, the more it will bring clarity and purpose in what you are trying to achieve. Set your sights on what you want. Give all of your energy and focus into making a change. Decide now to begin reprograming your thought process. It is your decision!

2. Make a commitment to yourself that you will move forward. Fear and doubt will be your first hurdle to overcome. Fear of rejection, fear of failure, success, and pain. If you do nothing, fear will win, and you will remain paralyzed in your desire to move forward. The only way to deal with fear is to face it head-on. The fear of a failed decision is always in the back of your mind. However, if you do fail in the process, you are not a failure. Remember, failure is an education. If you do something and it does not work out, you will know what doesn't work. You will be more educated and informed

to not make the same mistake the next time. As a result, you are better off than before, and you are making progress in your insight and maturity. Commit to overcoming negativity. Commit to a better life. Always demand more of yourself.

3. Once you have decided to move forward in overcoming roadblocks with reprograming your mind, resolve that this will be an ongoing approach to dealing with challenges in your life. Remember, you are never 100 percent in control. Take time to think through your life thus far. It has not always gone according to plan, and you had to be flexible and make adjustments along the way. You have learned from your mistakes, embraced failure, and overcome it, and challenged negative thinking for a better way of life. If you are making progress, you are going in the right direction. Any roadblock becomes an opportunity for you to pivot and find a new creative solution. You have the power and the mindset to make positive changes in your life.

   o *Empower yourself* by believing in yourself. You have the capacity to change!

   o *Surround yourself* with close friends and colleagues who have a healthy perspective on life, uplifting books, positive media of all forms, and music that builds you up and supports your positive outlook on life. Be on guard for information you get from outside sources that negatively influences your emotions and how you approach your life and career. Social media can be you best friend or your worst enemy. Avoid negativity. Attract positive energy.

- ○ *Visualize and see yourself* making changes and getting what you desire out of life. Live your life's plan, your dream!

Before their success, some of the world's most highly successful people experienced epic roadblocks and failures. We celebrate their success and enjoy what they have contributed to our society and us personally, but we often overlook the path that got them there—a path often marked with failure.

A lot of people fear the word *failure*, and it seems like everybody wants to achieve success in an instant. However, failure is something everybody experiences, and it's not always a bad thing. It just proves that the way to success is not easy. In fact, it is a vital experience that will make you rethink your priorities.

Get motivated and accept failure as merely a chance to learn. When you understand that failure is an inspiration behind success, you can start unlocking your potential.

Here are fifteen successful people who failed (a couple of times) before they were recognized by their glorious success! It's from "15 Highly Successful People Who Failed Before Succeeding" by Sebastian Kipman, entrepreneur and communications expert, www. lifehack.org.

Sir James Dyson

You know that frustrating feeling when you don't get something on the first attempt?

Multiply that by 5,126 because that's the number of failed prototypes Sir James Dyson went through over the course of 15 years before creating the eponymous best-selling bagless vacuum cleaner that led to a net worth of $4.5 billion.

If he gave up every single time he failed, he would not have been a successful entrepreneur who has successfully manufactured some of the best household appliances.

Steven Spielberg

His cinematic output has grossed more than $9 billion and brought him three Academy Awards, but the master of the blockbuster was rejected TWICE by the University of Southern California's School of Cinematic Arts. Aside from that, this director also struggled with dyslexia which made it harder for him to cope with school.

To date, he has won 11 Emmys, 3 Oscars, and 7 Golden Globes, and he's one of the most successful directors of today's time.

As their way of saying "Oops, I guess we were wrong about you" the school built a building in honor of Spielberg.

Thomas Edison

In what might be at once the most discouraging statement and worst teaching practice of all time, Thomas Edison was told by his teachers he was "too stupid to learn anything."

Edison went on to hold more than 1,000 patents, including the phonograph and practical electric lamp. Death most likely spared his teachers the ignominy of their incorrect assessment. Edison is now known as one of the most successful inventors who ever lived, and his creations changed the lives of billions of people.

Walt Disney

Can you imagine your childhood without Disney? Well, it could easily have been if Walt had listened to his former newspaper editor. The editor told Walt he 'lacked imagination and had no good ideas. Undeterred, Old Walt went on to create the cultural icon that bears his name.

Disney's take on failure:

"I think it's important to have a good hard failure when you're young ... Because it makes you kind of aware of what can happen to you. Because of it I've never had any fear in my whole life when we've been near collapse and all of that. I've never been afraid."

If you feel like giving up, remind yourself of what Disney said.

Albert Einstein

Want to achieve success? Let Albert Einstein inspire you.

His name is synonymous with intelligence, yet it wasn't always that way for Albert Einstein. As a child he didn't start speaking until he was four, reading until he was seven, and was thought to be mentally handicapped. If he gave up and never persevered, his most important theories could not have been known.

He went on to win a Nobel Prize and altered the world's approach to physics. I guess he was just thinking of the right thing to say for those first four years ...

J.K. Rowling

Before there was a wizard, there was welfare. Rowling was a broke, depressed, divorced single mother simultaneously writing a novel while studying. It's hard to believe it but a lot of publishers rejected Harry Potter.

Now one of the richest women in the world, Rowling reflects on her early failures:

"It is impossible to live without failing at something, unless you live so cautiously that you might as well not have lived at all—in which case, you fail by default."

Abraham Lincoln

Lincoln's failures were broad and numerous. He achieved the unique feat of leaving for a war a captain and returning a private (the lowest military rank).

He next took failure in his stride during multiple failed business attempts. Undeterred, Lincoln marched into the political realm, where he launched several failed runs at political office before his ascendance to President.

He shared this quote about his failure:

"My great concern is not whether you have failed, but whether you are content with your failure."

Jerry Seinfeld

Before the show about nothing, Seinfeld was a young comedian on the stand-up circuit. His first time on stage didn't go so well. On seeing the audience, he froze and was booed and jeered off stage.

His choices: pack it in and accept comedy isn't his thing or return to the same stage the following night and have the audience in hysterics. He opted for the latter and went on to become one of the most successful comedians of all time.

Theodor Seuss Geisel

Known to generations as Dr Seuss, the much-loved children's author had his first book rejected by 27 different publishers.

According to him, he was on his way home to burn his manuscript when he ran into one of his Dartmouth classmates who eventually helped him to find a publisher for his book. Now, he's known as one of the best children's authors.

His books that weren't good enough for these publishers went on to sell more than 600 million copies worldwide.

Oprah Winfrey

She's a billionaire with her own TV channel and a penchant for giving away cars but Oprah Winfrey was fired from her first TV job as an anchor in Baltimore.

In 2013, Oprah reflected on her experiences during a Harvard commencement speech:

"There is no such thing as failure. Failure is just life trying to move us in another direction."

Creating your own TV channel is a sure way never to get fired again!

Stephen King

In another instance in the never-ending series "Book Publishers Making Dumb Decisions," mega novelist Stephen King had his first book *Carrie* rejected 30 times.

This iconic storyteller was even told by publishers that they are not interested in any kind of science fiction that touches on negative utopias because they do not sell.

Dejected, King dumped the book in the trash. His wife retrieved it and implored him to resubmit it which led to his first book deal and spawned his illustrious career.

Vincent Van Gogh

A Van Gogh painting will cost you upwards of $100 million nowadays. But in his lifetime, Vincent Van Gogh couldn't get rid of the things.

He sold just one painting, "The Red Vineyard," during his lifetime, and the sale came not long before his death. Unfortunately for Vincent, others got to enjoy the financial spoils of his lifetime of toils.

According to this artist:

"Success is sometimes the outcome of a whole string of failures."

Elvis Presley

"You ain't goin' nowhere, son. You ought to go back to drivin' a truck."

These are the words that greeted Elvis Presley after his first performance at the Grand Ole Opry, after which he was promptly fired. Disposing of the keys to the truck, Presley went on to become the world's biggest star with a legacy that endures.

Michael Jordan

Either he was part of the greatest high school roster of all time, or his coach made a huge mistake in cutting Michael Jordan from his high school basketball team. Six Championships and five MVPs later, Jordan became arguably the greatest basketball player of all time.

Jordan famously said:

"I have missed more than 9,000 shots in my career. I have lost almost 300 games. On 26 occasions I have been entrusted to take the game winning shot, and I missed. I have failed over and over and over again in my life. And that is why I succeed."

Charles Darwin

The man credited with much of how we came to understand the world today, Darwin was considered an average student and abandoned a career in medicine as a result.

Darwin embarked on a lifetime study of nature that led to the seminal "On the Origin of Species" and forever altered the way humankind looks at our existence.

"10 Lessons We Can Learn from Failure" —
www.powerofpositivity.com,
published July 1, 2015, modified January 2, 2020:

Failing Builds Character—There is a lesson to be learned from everything, including failing. Perhaps the greatest benefit from failure is strength. Think about it. If life were perfect and every endeavor ended in seamless success, what sort of person would you be? The truth is—failure teaches us more about ourselves and builds character better than success ever could.

Failure Creates Opportunity—Think about this: how many times in your life have you failed at something only to discover another opportunity? Maybe it was a failed relationship that led you to someone great. Maybe it was a job that didn't suit you and brought you a better one. Regardless of what your circumstance was, the sweetness afterward was much better as a result, wasn't it?

Failure Is A Great Teacher—Failure was a way of showing what your strengths and weaknesses are while motivating you to correct them. In any area of life—academics, work, play, relationships, etc.—failure is often the driving force behind success. For example, Michael Jordan, arguably the greatest basketball player in history, failed to make his high school basketball team. When asked about his early failures, Jordan said: "I've failed over and over and over again in my life and that's why I succeed."

Failure Instills Courage—As should be clear by now, most people are scared of failure. Many of us are unwilling to take the uncertain path; we'd just prefer to stay in the same boat and not rock it too much. After all, we have responsibilities and people that depend on us. In short, failure requires courage. Whether the failure experienced was anticipated or not, you'll need to toughen up a bit to get through it.

Failure Teaches Perseverance—When experiencing failure, it's very easy to roll over and give up. "What's the use?" you say to yourself. It takes guts and determination to keep driving forward. Take J.K. Rowling, the author of the enormously successful *Harry Potter* series. Rowling said that she received "loads" of rejection letters over a five-year span before finding a publisher for one of the most successful book [and movie] series ever.

Failure Spawns Creativity—If necessity is the mother of invention, failure is the father. Nothing spurs creativity like failure. Artists and creators of all stripes know that if something doesn't work out, they must tap into their large reservoir of creative talent to create something truly unique.

Failure Requires Motivation—Winston Churchill once said, "Success is your ability to go from failure to failure without losing your enthusiasm." The most successful people are simply the ones who didn't give up. Finding the motivation to believe in yourself and press on is paramount.

Failure Is Acceptable—While a simple concept, accepting failure can be difficult to truly embrace. In the midst of experiencing failure, it is never a good feeling. In fact, this feeling can be downright gut-wrenching. But just remember that failure is acceptable ... lack of effort is not. Here's Michael Jordan again: "I can accept failure; everyone fails at something. But I can't accept not trying."

Failure Encourages Exploration—Steve Jobs knew that the corporate world was not for him. In fact, many things were not. He disliked college, societal norms, and the stiffness of business-people. Before founding Apple with Steve Wozniak, Jobs could have been labeled as a failure ... he just didn't care. Jobs said: "remembering that you are going to die is the best way I know to avoid the trap of thinking you have something to lose. You are already naked. There is no reason not to follow your heart." So, explore and don't let anything, especially fear of failure, stop you.

Failure Teaches Resilience—Along with making us better people, failing both teaches and strengthens resilience. Through the discomfort and uncertainty of an epic failure, one will be better able to take on any of life's challenges as they come. Resilience is something required of all successful people, and there is no better teacher of resilience than failure.

Final Thoughts

The famous and highly successful people's crowning achievements stem from drive and determination as much as ability.

Persistence and certitude are the difference between success and failure. So, if you want to succeed, don't be afraid to fail.

Fail often, fail fast and learn from your mistakes. The more times you fail, the closer you're getting to success.

We hope the lives of successful people who failed on their way to success has helped inspire you to strive more.

Roadblocks and failures are a reality, and you will face challenges from time to time in your life. Never, never, never give up!

As American writer Elbert Hubbard once said, "There is no failure except in no longer trying."

Avoid Burnout

Leadership is an active role; "lead" is a verb. But the leader who tries to do it all is headed for burnout, and in a powerful hurry.
—Bill Owens

I have a theory that burnout is about resentment. And you beat it by knowing what it is you're giving up that makes you resentful.
—Marissa Mayer

That's the thing: You don't understand burnout unless you've been burned out. And it's something you can't even explain. It's just doing something you have absolutely no passion for.
—Elena Delle Donne

Burnout!

What is burnout anyway? It's just an emotional problem. *Merriam-Webster* defines burnout as "exhaustion of physical or emotional strength or motivation usually as a result of prolonged stress or frustration."

Burnout occurs due to many reasons:

- Lack of rest or rejuvenation—being overworked.
- Lack of motivation or reward.
- Lack of control over your work.
- Work does not suit our skills or interests.
- Unchallenging or monotonous work.
- Work environment is highly political.
- Work culture is not aligned with our values.
- We have too many emergencies demanding our time at work and at home.
- We are not well, or a family member is sick.

I am sure there are many other reasons for burnout, but most people can relate to the points listed above. How about you? The question then is, how do you prevent burnout?

Here are some suggestions:

1. *Take time-outs.* Start your day in a meditative state. Healthy self-talk addressing your positive attributes and expressing gratitude for your life, family, friends, and accomplishments always helps to start your day. This provides emotional balance for the beginning of your day. And when you have moments in your day that seem overwhelming, take a walk, take in your surroundings, find your inner peace, and then return to your work environment. When we walk, we tend to work through problems, emotions, and circumstances that affect our mood.

2. *Take care of your body physically.* Your energy level will be higher if you get a good night's sleep. David Perlmutter, MD, board-certified neurologist, and Austin Perlmutter, MD, board-certified internal medicine physician, state in their recent book, *BRAIN WASH—Detox Your Mind for Clearer Thinking, Deeper relationships and Lasting Happiness*:

    > Sleep is critical to our ability to handle emotional stressors. By studying sleep's characteristic brain waves throughout its various stages during the night, scientists have shown that one stage in particular—REM sleep—is a key promoter of healthy emotional regulation.
    >
    > Bottom line: poor sleep may make us more emotionally reactive. Detaching us from the ability to make rational, optimal decisions. And what are the downstream effects of this? Likely stress and an

obesity-inducing diet, both in turn keep us from getting good sleep.

Have an exercise program that you maintain on a consistent basis, keep hydrated, and practice mindful eating. An occasional detox or the practice of intermittent fasting may prove beneficial.

3. *Don't be afraid to say no.* Learn to cut back on commitments that are too draining. Sometimes you just have to decline the offer to participate in an organization and/or activity. By cutting back, you contribute more effectively when you are not so overwhelmed and overcommitted.

4. *Research for solutions.* If there are some areas you want to engage in, go to the internet and do your research. Find the best and most efficient solutions to career choices and relationship issues.

5. *Organize your plan.* Make a list of areas in your life you want to work on and set priorities for them. People always fail because they fail to plan. So, plan!

6. *Upgrade your skills.* The workplace is ever changing. Technology is outpacing our ability to compete and be successful. Seek out opportunity to obtain needed skills, certifications, and any additional education needed. The decision is yours!

7. *Determine what is most important to you.* Spend more time on your high-value activities and therefore increase your life satisfaction.

8. *Practice mindfulness.* Mindfulness is the act of focusing on your breath flow and being intensely aware of what you are sensing and feeling in every moment, without interpretation or judgment. In a career setting, this practice involves facing situations with openness and patience and without judgment. Keep an open mind as you consider your options. Try not to let a demanding or unrewarding job undermine your health.

9. *Treat burnout as a lifelong concern.* Always be sensitive to not overcommitting. Balance out your life and always be on guard.

10. *Time for a change.* Sometimes it is time for a change in career, different industry, or different company—possibly a new career path that requires education, training, and new skills. Your mind, body, and spirit can only take so much stress and discontentment in your professional life. Change can be the solution. You get a fresh start and make better choices based on your prior experience.

Believe in yourself and your abilities. It's important to identify what you need from your work, sometimes even before you decide to make a change or take a job offer. Knowing exactly what you need from your career will help you confidently make decisions about it.

Having other interests outside of work is a great way to prevent yourself from getting too focused on your job. Other interests help you to escape from the pressures of work. Take on a new sport, enroll in a cooking class, take a course in photography, or volunteer for a nonprofit organization. These are only a few examples. Similarly, self-care is crucial to preventing workplace burnout. If you're taken care of, you are more likely to be able to cope with the stress of your career. If you have difficulty in coping, it may be advisable for you to seek the professional help of a psychologist or licensed professional counselor.

Workplace burnout is a common thing for many people, but it doesn't have to be. You can work to prevent or treat workplace burnout and have a career that you find fulfilling and enjoyable.

What are some activities that you enjoy that would help you avoid burnout?

1. _____

2. _____

3. _____

4. _____

5. _____

Successful Selling—Your Brand

Whether you think you can or you think you can't—you're right.
— Henry Ford

Selling yourself is more involved than just speaking the right words. It's about having the right air about you. You might say that you are not a salesperson. You are 100 percent wrong. How you are perceived in every encounter in life is related to your ability to project a positive and engaging personality. In essence, you are your own brand.

You desire people to like you, enjoy your company, and, as the opportunity presents itself, do business with you. All healthy business engagements are based on developed relationships. In a business setting, aside from your hard skills, people hire you and do business with you because they like you.

So how do you make that first impression?

Do your homework. Use the internet and social media to find out all you can about the person you will be meeting—their background, shared interests, their accomplishments, and so on. How do they appear visually on social media and various sites on the internet?

First: The Look

Dress appropriately for professional encounters. Business casual is the best approach.

> *Style is a reflection of your attitude and your personality.*
> —Shawn Ashmore

Men: If you are too formal (suit, tie, designer clothing and shoes), you will be too overpowering for the other person to relate to. If underdressed (casual shirt, jeans, and boots), they might not take you seriously. Basic conservative attire is always in order: shirt, slacks, sport coat, and polished shoes or appropriate casual footwear—not sandals. If you don't have a sport coat, a basic navy blazer is always a winner. If no sport coat or blazer, a compromise would be a solid navy suit without a tie. In all cases, no large pattern fabrics, plaids, or bold colors. No tattoos visible please.

Women: Conservative business suit, skirt and blouse, or conservative dress. Again, no bold colors, patterns, or plaids. Minimal accessories. They tend to distract. Women tend to be more conscious of their dress and appearance and understand what a conservative presence is all about. You never want to be overdressed or present yourself as overpowering.

Summary: In a professional environment, you meet people on their level, congruent with their company setting, surroundings, and protocols. Anything otherwise will not result in a good outcome.

Having said that, if you are in a high-fashion career position, conservative appearance may not be applicable. In those cases, dress according to the fashion dictates of the position you are seeking. As many designers have stated, a simple, understated black dress for women with minimal accessories is always a good option.

Appropriate dress exudes confidence and gives a great initial impression.

Second: Your Presence

Body language speaks volumes. Standing upright, eyes fixed on the other person—eye to eye—hand extended for a handshake, and a warm smile. Sit as directed and engage in conversation. Never let your eyes wander left to right as if you are looking for answers. Answer directly. Keep your hands in your lap or crossed on the table. Many people tend to mover their hands a lot in a meeting, which distracts from communication interchange. You may need to practice in a mirror as if you are in a meeting or in an interview, making sure your hands and eyes are not a distraction. This is a common problem. Most people are not aware of their body language. Nonverbal communication tells people more about you than anything. Nonverbals sell you more than anything else.

Body language is a very powerful tool. We had body language before we had speech, and apparently, 80% of what you understand in a conversation is read through the body, not the words.
—Deborah Bull

Get in touch with the way the other person feels. Feelings are 55% body language, 38% tone, and 7% words.
—Deborah Bull

Being a great leader starts with looking people in the eye. After all, if you can't connect with people, you can't convince people of your beliefs. If you can't convince people of your beliefs, they won't follow you. If they won't follow you, you can't become a leader. Eye contact matters!
—Deborah Bull

Answer questions directly. Do not embellish the conversation. If the other party asks an open-ended question that calls for further information, proceed to give more details. Listen more, speak less. Be specific in your responses. If you have common interests, that makes for relating to the other person; take advantage and explore that common ground. That makes for a common platform for constructive communication. Always get back to the point of the engagement.

Never memorize and give a scripted response. That is a dead giveaway that you are not real. People relate to real people who can speak directly to them, seek common interests, and get to the point of what they want to achieve. If you speak script, you are boring, and people will not believe you. Speak from your experience, what you truly believe in—who you are and what your product or service provides. If it comes across as heartfelt, they will believe you.

Third: The Message

Remember, you are in a meeting to provide solutions. People don't want to have a rehash of your career path, commonly referred to as *résumé speak*. You are to provide them solutions for them personally or their company.

Never downgrade your competition. Acknowledge your competition with respect but communicate your differences and the additional value your product or service brings to the relationship.

Never promote what you can't deliver. Set realistic expectations.

Cut out negative self-talk. Don't be hard on yourself. Don't compare yourself to others. You need to convey confidence in your ability to communicate effectively to get the results you want. If you have to fake it until you make it, that's what you do. Remember, you are your brand. You are selling yourself first. The resulting sale, new job opportunity, or new professional relationship is the result of you promoting your brand—you!

Don't be a VICTIM of negative self-talk—remember YOU are listening.
—Bob Proctor

Turn off any self-talk that tells you that you are
destined to live a small life. You're not.
—Loral Langemeier

You open the door to new opportunities and sales and closed deals. You are your own pathway to success or failure. You only fail when you allow fear, weakness, and low self-esteem to take control. You are better than any failure; you are success!

Fourth: In Summary

What I have discovered in this journey is that the keys to success in your personal and professional lives are the same. You cannot separate them. They are all interrelated. As we have discussed in this book, there are different ways to define success, but the success principles are the same. For purposes of emphasis and a good summary, here they are:

- *Be honest always.* That's with yourself and others. Your integrity is your most important asset. It is hard to establish and easy to lose.
- *Be clear with your communications.* Clarify your thoughts mentally, write them down, and think before you speak.
- *Keep it simple.* Fewer concise words are more powerful than long dissertations. When you embellish your comments with massive detail, you overpower the other person. They don't really hear what you are saying.

- *Listen more.* The one with the most power in the room is the person who listens well and offers input after considering the other comments.
- *Accept responsibility.* If you make a mistake, own it and admit it. Apologize if appropriate. Take action to correct the mistake and seek a solution going forward.
- *Keep your commitments.* Be cautious about what you commit to. Set realistic expectations and deliverables that can be met.
- *Work hard.* There is no substitution for hard work. Embrace opportunity. Focus intently on doing quality work. Go beyond the norm. Do the exceptional!
- *Ask questions.* There is no better way to grow in your personal and professional lives than to seek answers to questions you have in your life and career. Knowledge is power. So get as much power as you need to succeed!
- *Collaborate.* Find ways to help others succeed. Be a team player. This is the role of a true leader. Remember, leadership is a role you assume, not a job title.
- *Be prepared.* Before any interaction or meeting, do your research. Have questions and seek meaningful answers that you and others will benefit from.
- *Have a vision.* Know where you are going. Have a life plan that makes sense and has the possibility of becoming a reality. If you cannot see it, it may never happen. Practice visualization and see yourself in that particular role.
- *Set goals.* There can never be true success in life if you do not set goals. Make sure they are not unreasonable and can be achieved within a realistic timeframe. They are usually

a part of a life plan, which includes your career, education, faith, family, acquiring assets, and building long-term relationships.

- *Build networks.* We are created for relationships. No matter how intelligent or smart you think you are, you will never be able to achieve your full potential without support and help from others. Make the effort to connect with like-minded people. Engage in mastermind groups. Develop strong social networks that support your career and values.
- *Never stop learning.* Continue to develop skills, knowledge, attitudes, and competence in your life. Read and study everything relating to your career path. Study about the most successful people in your career field, both locally and nationally. Find out what makes them successful and apply those lessons to your own life. On a personal level, seek knowledge on how to have healthy personal relationships and a meaningful spiritual life. In all of these areas, personal and professional learning bring balance and meaning to your life.

Winning perceptions to sustain leadership and success in your professional and personal life:

- likeable
- trustworthy
- dependable
- consistent
- reliable

7

A WINNING
METHODOLOGY

*You were born to win, but to be a winner, you must
plan to win, prepare to win, and expect to win.*
—Zig Ziglar

*The winner's edge is not in a gifted birth, a high IQ, or in talent. The
winner's edge is in attitude, not aptitude. Attitude is the criterion for success.*
—Denis Waitley

*To be a consistent winner means preparing not just one day,
one month or even one year—but for a lifetime.*
—Bill Rodgers

One of the best resources for understanding success is to ask a successful professional about their definition of success and what resources and/or events in their career made them successful. How did they adapt, manage, and lead others? Under their leadership, how did they create value for their company and shareholders?

One such individual is Mr. Scott Boxer. Mr. Boxer was president and CEO of Service Experts, was former president of Lennox Industries, and held various senior leadership roles at York International. Mr. Boxer currently serves on the board of directors for EnTouch Controls, Richardson, Texas.

Mr. Boxer attributes his success in part to the Hedgehog Concept, as presented by Tom Collins in his book *Good to Great* (Harper Collins Publishers, NYC). With permission, I share this concept as presented by Mr. Collins:

The Hedgehog Concept

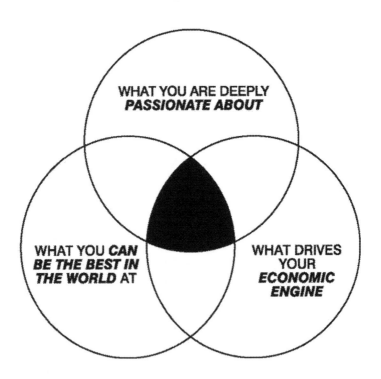

BILL BLALOCK

The Hedgehog Concept is a simple, crystalline concept that flows from deep understanding about the intersection of three circles: 1) what you are deeply passionate about, 2) what you can be the best in the world at, and 3) what best drives your economic or resource engine. Transformations from good to great come about by a series of good decisions made consistently with a Hedgehog Concept, supremely well executed, accumulating one upon another, over a long period of time.

Excerpts from *Good to Great:*

Are you a hedgehog or a fox? In his famous essay "The Hedgehog and the Fox," Isaiah Berlin divided the world into hedgehogs and foxes, based upon an ancient Greek parable: "The fox knows many things, but the hedgehog knows one big thing."

Those who built the good-to-great companies were, to one degree or another, hedgehogs. They used their hedgehog nature to drive toward what we came to call a Hedgehog Concept for their companies. Those who led the comparison companies tended to be foxes, never gaining the clarifying advantage of a Hedgehog Concept, being instead scattered, diffused, and inconsistent.

For the comparison companies, the exact same world that had become so simple and clear to the good-to-great companies remained complex and shrouded in mist. Why? For two reasons. First, the comparison companies never asked the right questions, the questions prompted by the three circles. Second, they set their goals and strategies *more from bravado than from understanding.*

A Hedgehog Concept is not a goal to be the best, a strategy to be the best, an intention to be the best, a plan to be the best. It is an *understanding* of what you *can* be the best at. The distinction is absolutely crucial.

Every company would like to be the best at something, but few actually understand—with piercing insight and egoless clarity—what they actually have the potential to be the best at and, just as important, what they *cannot* be the best at. And it is this distinction that stands as one of the primary contrasts between the good-to-great companies and the comparison companies.

To go from good to great requires transcending the curse of competence. It requires the discipline to say, "Just because we are good at it—just because we're making money and generating growth—doesn't necessarily mean we can become the best at it." The good-to-great companies understood that doing what you are good at will only make you good; focusing solely on what you can potentially do better than any other organization is the only path to greatness.

As you search for your own concept, keep in mind that when the good-to-great companies finally grasped their Hedgehog Concept, it had none of the tiresome, irritating blasts of mindless bravado typical of the comparison companies. "Yep, we could be the best at that" was stated as the recognition of a fact, no more startling than observing that the sky is blue, or the grass is green. When you get your Hedgehog Concept right, it has the quiet ping of truth, like a single, clear, perfectly struck note hanging in the air in the hushed silence of a full auditorium at the end of a quiet movement of a Mozart piano concerto. There is no need to say much of anything; the quiet truth speaks for itself.

The Hedgehog Concept has application in successful organizations; however, a focused management philosophy is another key element that Mr. Boxer ascribes to. To quote Mr. Boxer:

I have found in my career that great leadership had certain philosophies that they demonstrated without ever knowing how to describe them, but they operated to them and were very successful in many different situations. It wasn't until I read the book "Good to Great" that I could understand what great leaders did instinctively that I could articulate them. Let me describe 3 of them.

First Who … Then What

If we get the right people on the bus, the right people in the right seats, and the wrong people off the bus, then we will figure out how to take it somewhere great.

Confront the Brutal Facts

When you start an honest and diligent effort to determine the truth of your situation, the right decisions often become self-evident. The key is creating a culture where people have an opportunity to be heard, and ultimately for the truth to be heard. Creating the climate of a safe environment where truth can be heard takes constant work.

<u>The Hedgehog Concept</u> [described within in this section]

Aligned with Mr. Boxers comments, we must always provide a safe work environment where people can freely exchange new ideas and approaches, creating new opportunities and solving business challenges. Each employee is to be valued and viewed as a contributing factor to the company's success. Safe work environments create and sustain a culture where innovation and competitiveness thrive to serve the best interest of employees as well as the products and services a company provides.

8

THE FUTURE

You can't connect the dots looking forward; you can only connect them looking backwards. So, you have to trust that the dots will somehow connect in your future. You have to trust in something— your gut, destiny, life, karma, whatever. This approach has never let me down, and it has made all the difference in my life.
—Steve Jobs

The Future—Your Future

As we look to the future, unlimited possibilities exist with the further development of artificial intelligence, advanced manufacturing, the metaverse, virtual reality, and quantum computing. These areas of development will be in the forefront of developing products and services that will impact our lives forever. They will require continuing advancements in software development, machine learning, and engineering disciplines, all of which will demand continued learning. They will impact your customer/client relationships and product and service offerings as you go through your life and career.

Professor John McCarthy coined the term "artificial intelligence" in 1956 at Dartmouth College at the first ever AI conference. Later that year, JC Shaw, Herbert Simon, and Allen Newell created the first AI software program named "Logic Theorist."

Artificial intelligence (AI) and its subset, machine learning, will change the work environment and customer/client engagement.

AI uses algorithms to imitate our human brain functions. AI uses decision trees and logic theories to find the best possible solution to a given problem or request. AI includes predictive modeling to predict events based on previous and current data. Examples would be calling your airline for flight information, a specific customer service, or your credit card provider. In some cases, it will recognize who you are by your phone number and then proceed to update you immediately or direct you via a "call attendant" for selecting options to solve your inquiry. In these cases, you are not talking to a human; you are talking to an intelligent computer that is assisting you. There is limited human intervention.

Further examples where AI is utilized include automation, self-driving cars, robotics, and advanced manufacturing.

Paul R. Daugherty and H. James Wilson, in their book *Human + Machine—Reimagining Work in the Age of AI* (Harvard Business Review Press, 2018), say there are five key steps, referred to as MELDS, for reimaging business processes in the AI age.

Mindset

Experimentation

Leadership

Data

Skills

Executives must adopt the proper mindset, with a focus on not just improving business processes but rather on completely reimagining business processes and the way that work is performed.

Executives need to foster a culture of AI experimentation that allows them to quickly realize how and where the technology can change a process, and where it makes sense to increase scale and scope of a process.

Executives must exercise the proper leadership in promoting responsible AI and managing trust, legal, and ethical concerns that accompany AI by considering the societal consequences of some process changes.

Executives need to recognize the critical importance of data, not just their firm's own AI-enabling data but also the broader landscape of available data.

Executives need to recognize the needed skills to achieve a robust AI environment. We infer here "infusion skills," the combination of human and machine capabilities that enable firms to reimagine processes. This will have a direct impact on the future of work.

Machine learning (ML) goes a step further.

The computer itself learns without being programed on a regular basis. ML trains the computer to think on its own. Machine learning is a subset of artificial intelligence. Online recommendation and facial recognition are examples of ML.

On the horizon are two types of AI:

- *Theory of mind*: The computer will understand human reasoning and motives. It will need fewer examples to learn because it understands motives and has been building that data over many years. This is the next evolution in AI.
- *Self-awareness*: The computer possesses human-level intelligence that can bypass human intelligence. The machine has a sense of self-consciousness. This does not exist currently. But it is definitely on the horizon.

Quantum computing is expected to disrupt a wide range of industries in the next 10–20 years, though the specific time frame strongly depends upon scientific and engineering results. Currently we have several market forecasts, though it is important to understand the high degree of uncertainty within this field.

Market Reports World, for example, states that the quantum computing market will grow by $7.3b during 2021–2025, with a compound annual growth rate [CAGR] of 19%.

Meanwhile, research and Markets valued the quantum computing software market at $472m in 2021 and predicted it will grow to $1.8b by 2026. This effectively demonstrates the variability in market forecasts." ("Who Is Responsible for the Quantum Leap" by Daniel Shaposhnikov, April 29, 2021, Phystech Ventures.)

In 2019, The Boston Consulting Group (BCG) prepared its vision, which identifies three phases of development in quantum computing technology (see article "Where Will Quantum Computers Create Value—and When?" May 13, 2019, by Matt Langione, Corbin Tillemann-Dick, Amit Kumar, and Vikas Taneja):

1. The Noisy Intermediate-Scale Quantum [NISQ]—Using scientific and Specialized applications, NISQ devices are capable of performing useful, discrete functions, but are also characterized by high error rates that limit functionality. Error correction therefore will likely remain quantum computing's biggest challenge for the better part of the decade.

2. Experts then predict the development of a quantum advantage phase in 10–20 years, which can lead to a potential economic impact of 25–50 billion. This era will be characterized by quantum computers achieving superior performance in industrial tasks. Specifically, increases in speed, cost and quality are expected.

3. The final phase will be marked by the development of full-scale, fault-tolerant quantum computers, which will almost certainly disrupt a wide range of industries. Experts predict this will occur in roughly 20 years. Problems with scale and stability will also be solved.

Major technology firms are in the forefront of quantum technology research and development, including IBM, Microsoft, Google (Alphabet), Intel, Honeywell, D-Wave Systems, and QC Ware. Knowing what we know about these firms and how they have impacted our lives in the past and present, it is clear that with the advent of quantum computing, our lives will be constantly changing in the future. New innovative career opportunities are surfacing in this space.

Quantum computing is pioneering and can analyze and find solutions, cognitive and otherwise, that will revolutionize our world.

Because of the high-level intelligence of these computer systems, many programs that are currently encrypted for security or confidentiality reasons will have to be updated to ensure that they cannot be unlocked, with information exposed that would otherwise be protected.

The metaverse expands our ability to communicate!

In 2021, Facebook was renamed Meta Platforms, and its chairman, Mark Zuckerberg, declared a company commitment to developing a metaverse. Many of the virtual reality technologies by Meta Platforms remain to be developed. But metaverse is already here with virtual avatars and meetings held in virtual reality. Future applications of metaverse technology include work productivity, interactive learning environments, e-commerce, real estate, and fashion.

The CEO of Accenture, Julie Sweet, has recently stated that they use the metaverse extensively in their organization to facilitate better communication abilities, especially in virtual and hybrid team meetings. The metaverse will continue to evolve and will impact how we communicate in the future.

Virtual reality (VR) is here!

VR is a simulated experience that can be similar to or completely different from the real world. The most relatable usage of VR today is in video games. Applications for careers today and in the future will be in education (i.e., medical or military training) and in business, such as business meetings and conferences.

As you can see, technology will continue to be in the forefront of shaping our world and how we relate to one another in our personal and professional lives. This is the foundation for the future. Each of these concepts will revolutionize every aspect of our lives. Careers in this field will require constant learning and certifications to remain competitive.

IQ + EQ + DQ

Successful leaders today and in the future must possess triple-threat leadership capability: IQ + EQ + DQ. They must possess a combination of two familiar attributes, intellect (IQ) and emotional intelligence (EQ), plus a third strategic element, DQ, which is interpreted in two ways in the business environment: elevated decency and digital quotient, a.k.a. digital transformation. The first is addressing the human elements of organizational dynamics and how people relate to one another and the business, and the second is the emergence of digital technology and its impact on the future of business operations and human intervention.

The Decency Quotient

In a recent article by Bill Boulding, dean of Duke University's Fuqua School of Business, Bill stated the following:

> A decency quotient, or DQ, goes a step further than EQ. DQ implies a person has not only empathy for employees and colleagues but also the genuine desire to care for them.

DQ means wanting something positive for everyone in the workplace and ensuring everyone feels respected and valued.

Ajay Banga, the CEO of Mastercard, was the first person to tell me about DQ, in a talk in front of students at Duke University's Fuqua School of Business. "IQ is important; EQ is really important. What matters to me is DQ," Banga explained. "If you can bring your decency quotient to work every day, you will make the company a lot of fun for people—and people will enjoy being there and doing the right thing."

Technology, innovation, and automation are changing the very nature of work. Innovation brings about innovative solutions that leave many people out of the workforce. Leaders must be sensitive to the impact of the digital revolution and make provision to provide training and services to employees as they transition to the new work environment. In some cases, management will need to provide outplacement services and exit strategies to facilitate this paradigm shift. It takes strong leadership and resolve to do the right thing when it comes to managing human capital.

The Digital Quotient

Digital Quotient (DQ) is a "shorthand" metaphor for a skill that is growing increasingly important: to understand organizations digital maturity and how that relates to a specific business needs or opportunities. Leaders must understand digital strengths and weaknesses, be aware of technologies that can elevate the business, know what works and what does not, be keenly aware of emerging technologies, and be focused on digital strategies that will have the best impact on the business over the long term. Keep in mind that "what works" is constantly changing, rapidly, as technology continues to evolve.

Digital transformation is the process of using digital technologies to create new—or modify existing—business processes, culture, and customer experiences to meet changing business and market requirements. This is reimagining business, transitioning from analogue to digital on a global basis.

Chris Moye, a successful CEO, former Chief Transformation Officer at McKinsey and VP at IBM has a unique background and perspective on what it takes to successfully implement an analog-to-digital transformation. In a recent interview with Greg Selker, Managing Director and the North American Technology Practice Leader at Stanton Chase, Chris shares his perspective:

"I think it's important to know that if you want results, you will need to make some changes in the culture – and this takes time. Therefore, you need to think ahead and be prepared to "walk your talk" – to model the new behaviors that are needed. Some think company culture doesn't have a lot of hard business value. I beg to differ. It means getting people, over time, to align on values; the "why,", the "how," and the "what" of the business. This is very important because analog to digital transformation means redefining "work" throughout the organization. So, it necessarily goes deep and, in my experience, is fundamental to leading change"

The first phase of digital transformation is to align senior leaders and to have a series of focused discussions on business drivers and values. Mindsets, processes, and behaviors are how you change a culture. Remember, to effect digital transformation, it is essential that people's habits and behaviors are changed. As mentioned previously, the process is not accomplished overnight. It requires a dedicated senior leadership team, a playbook, and a commitment to building trust.

Chris is currently an "executive in residence" at a large, well-known PE group. That said, he is someone who tends to find interesting situations, and given the disruption in our lives and economy today, I suspect he will end up in another CEO role, or in a position that allows him an opportunity to leverage his skills and interest in Digital Transformation, a powerful force that is remaking companies and entire industries before our eyes.

As you explore career options, the area of Digital Transformation is an area that should be considered. After all, we are living in a digital world, and it is through DQ that future leaders will excel.

Other areas of transformation:

We have already addressed artificial intelligence (AI), machine learning (ML), quantum computing, the meta universe, and virtual reality (VR). We now need to further define some additional areas of transformation that are strategic to digital transformation as we look to the future:

The Internet of Things (IoT)

These are objects and devices equipped with sensors that collect and transmit data over the internet. IoT devices are where digital technology meets physical reality. Applications like supply chain logistics and self-driving cars generate real-time data that AI and big data analytics applications turn into automation and decisions.

Blockchain

Blockchain is a distributed, permanent ledger or record of electronic transactions. Blockchain provides total transaction transparency to those who require it and is inaccessible to those who do not. Organizations are using blockchain as a foundation for super-resilient supply chain and cross-border financial services transformations.

IBM defines Blockchain as a shared, immutable ledger that facilitates the process of recording transactions and tracking assets in a business network. An asset can be tangible (a house, car, cash, land) or intangible (intellectual property, patents, copyrights, branding).

Digitization

Digitization is the conversion of paper-based information into digital data. This process is a constant within every industry. It is pivotal in transformation initiatives in health care (electronic medical records), government, education, and many business enterprises. It is the progression from analogue to digital data.

The use of technology and the utilization of human capital in a digital age is essential to the future of business as well as enhancing our personal lives. Many of these processes are already in motion in our society and will only accelerate in the future.

Future leaders need to have an understanding and, in many cases, a working knowledge of these processes to achieve optimum success in their careers and personal lives.

FINAL THOUGHTS

Personalize the Experience

With technology driving change, there will always be situations where you are required to interact with your peers, team, and senior-level management in a corporate setting, or as head of your own company, or as a self-employed individual. Human intervention will always be required in person or via text, email, Zoom, Skype, or a phone call. I am sure, over time, there will be other innovative means by which we continue the personal connection. But we must continue to make connections to elevate our life experiences.

It is essential that you are aware of technology advances and that you know how they are applied in the work environment.

The future is in your hands. The decisions you make are yours. *Mastermind Your Life* is only a guide and resource as you go through life. Everyone wants to be successful. As we have pointed out in this book, success is defined in many ways. Find your own path to success, which has many dimensions—personal and professional. Utilize all the tools, resources, and training that you can.

At the end of the day, your life should have meaning and purpose. That's the ultimate in defining a successful life!

Seek Balance in Your Life

The challenge you face is finding a balance between technology and human connections. When are you missing the physical presence of connecting, communicating, and building relationships in person? Responding to an avatar or texting a message is a form of making a connection, but you are not intimately relating to the other person. There are always subtle nuances in body language, speech, and the feeling of presence with a real person. These are lacking when you totally rely on technically driven forms of connecting. As we have noted, with the advent of AI and other advanced means of communicating, you talk to a computer.

Voice identification is used by many institutions when you desire to access your accounts or information on your mobile device. That system application through AI uses your unique voice pattern to grant you access to your information,

Retina and fingerprint identification systems are also being used to access information that is specific to you as an individual.

These types of identification security systems are helpful in business and customer relationships; however, when we desire to communicate with another individual, it is ultimately essential that we engage with other people *in person* to establish, develop, and grow that real personal connection.

So, the challenge remains. Technology is a tool but not a replacement for human connectivity in meaningful relationships. Always be cognitively aware how technology is gradually taking control over your personal interactions. Seek balance and understand that advancements in the future are there to enhance your life, not to control it. If you do otherwise, you will give up your unique personality and the ability to have meaning and purpose in your personal and professional relationships.

Don't become just data; become a real person!

In order to achieve success, you must first be persistent.
—Brad Turnbull

Success is when you try to achieve your inward vision externally and have it come off the way you see it. Then YOU feel successful about it; that's how success is measured.
—George Lucas

ABOUT THE AUTHOR

Bill Blalock Jr. holds a Bachelor of Business Administration from Methodist University, Fayetteville, North Carolina, and a master's in counseling from Amberton University, Dallas, Texas. During his corporate career, he held many successful management positions at Frito-Lay, Coca-Cola Enterprises Inc., Ernst & Young, and Cadbury Schweppes, to mention a few.

After leaving corporate America, he focused on his passion for the development and enhancement of individual lives through his professional coaching practice. His aim has always been to provide solutions for success in his clients' personal and professional lives.

His first book, *Living Your Legacy Now—Inspiring Life Lessons for a Successful, Healthy, and Successful Life*, he made a positive impact on the lives of many people. *Mastermind Your Life* is Mr. Blalock's second book in his Legacy Series. His purpose in this book is to help individuals achieve personal and professional success and for organizations to continue to excel in offering exceptional products and services. He provides definitions of success at different levels and offers a path to achieve a successful outcome for the reader's life journey.

Mr. Blalock continues to help individuals and businesses create and maximize opportunities by staying focused, breaking barriers, and enjoying a greater quality of life.

Mr. Blalock has written many articles, has been interviewed on various media outlets, and has been a conference speaker and panelist, in addition to doing workshops and individual coaching.

For information about Mr. Blalock's availability:
www.billblalock.com
LinkedIn: linkedin.com/in/bill-blalock-42851913
Facebook: www.facebook.com/billblalockauthor
Email: bill@billblalock.com

SUGGESTED RESOURCES

Extreme Ownership—How Navy Seals Lead and Win by Jocko Willink and Leif Babin (St. Martin's Press, NYC).

From Impressed to Obsessed—12 Principles for Turning Customers and Employees into Lifelong Fans by Jon Picoult (McGraw Hill Books).

Good to Great—Why Some Companies Make the Leap ... and Others Don't by Jim Collins (HarperCollins Publishers Inc., NYC).

Human + Machine—Reimagining Work in the Age of AI by Paul R. Daugherty and H. James Wilson (Harvard Business Review Press, Boston, Massachusetts).

Leading at a Distance—Practical Lessons for Virtual Success by James M. Citrin and Darleen Derosa (John Wiley & Sons Inc., Hoboken, New Jersey).

Start with Why—How Great Leaders Inspire Everyone to Take Action by Simon Sinek (Penguin Books Ltd., London, England).

Printed in the United States
by Baker & Taylor Publisher Services